FRIDAY FACTS

An Interesting Book of Facts

BY R. S. ROGERS

DEDICATED TO MY MOTHER AND FATHER
Thank you for making life interesting

CreateSpace
[2018]

In 1895 there were only two cars in the entire State of Ohio and the drivers of those two cars crashed into one another

The original Ronald McDonald was fired for being overweight

If you spend one hour in a swimming pool you will intake about 50 ounces of urine

You can actually send a person or company a pile of shit in the mail (see shitsenders.com)

At the 1909 World's Fair in Seattle a one month old baby was given away in a raffle, no one knows what happened to him

There is no period in the 'S" of Harry S Truman because it doesn't stand for anything

When the Nebraska Cornhuskers play a sold out game in their stadium, that stadium becomes the third largest city in the state

 1/3 of all divorce filings in 2011 contained the word "face book"

There is a real team of Avengers. They were Jewish assassins who after WWII tracked down and killed Nazi war criminals

If you rub an onion slice on your foot, you will be able to taste it in your mouth in about 30-60 minutes

Crabs are now in Antarctic waters for the first time in 30 million years

Green house (CO2) gases hit a milestone of 400 parts per million

Benjamin Franklin actually wrote an essay titled "Fart Proudly"

Sweden recycles its garbage so well that it has run out of garbage, it now imports garbage from Norway

100 years from now there will be 500 million dead people on Face book

Astronauts in space cannot burp because there is no gravity to separate the liquids from the gases

Chocolate milk is proven to relieve muscle soreness after a workout

Japanese planes that attacked Pearl Harbor were manufactured by Mitsubishi

Red heads are less sensitive to electrically induced pain but more sensitive to thermal induced pain

The first man to survive a fall over Niagara Falls died later when he slipped on an orange peel

The first woman to be attacked in the movie Jaws was really screaming in pain. The harness she was hooked up to broke her hip

President John Quincy Adams kept a pet alligator in the East room of the White house

Australia is the only continent without an active volcano

Albert Einstein had his trash searched, mail opened and phone tapped by the FBI for 22 years

Only three types of animals form armies and go to war-- Humans, ants and crows

During WWII a Japanese man saved over 6,000 Jews by writing them all visas to Japan against Germanys' orders

Colombian Drug Lord Pablo Escobar was so rich he spent $2,500 a month on rubber bands to hold his cash

The US is 5% of the world's population and 25% of all prisoners in the world

More serial killers are born in the month of November than any other month

111,111,111 X 111,111,111 = 12,345,678,987,654,321

Whirligig beetles have two pairs of eyes, one pair is used for looking above water and one pair used for looking below

McDonalds is no longer the largest fast food chain, Subway now has more stores across the globe

In 1880 the Queen of Thailand drowned while her subjects watched because they were not allowed to touch her

John Cena has granted over 250 make-a-wish foundation wishes, that's more than anyone in history

Sunsets on Mars are blue

Venezuela has a never ending lightning storm that has been going on since the year 1595

The same man that created Wonder Woman is the same man that invented the lie detector

In 1918 Chicago more than 100 waiters were arrested for poisoning bad tippers

Female Jackie Mitchell once struck out Babe Ruth and Lou Gehrig back to back and was promptly banned from playing baseball

Until 1970 California born resident could attend any college in the University of California system for free

According to Congress pizza is considered a vegetable

A woman trying to commit suicide jumped from the Eiffel Tower, landed on a car and survived. She later married the owner of said car

The two highest IQs ever recorded belonged to women

During his presidency Franklin Pierce was arrested for running over a woman with his horse

In Denmark students get paid to go to school

While many Americans think violent crime is getting worse, they actually occur three times less than they did in the 1970s

A pineapple is not a single fruit but a group of berries fused together

Organized people are less likely to develop Alzheimer's disease

The Assassin Bug wears its victim's bodies as armor

In 2007 a Bosnian married couple found out that they had been cheating on each other in an online chatroom... with each other

The Netherlands recently closed eight prisons across the country because due to lack of crime

When South Park aired its Anti-Family Guy episode, the producers received flowers from the staff of the Simpsons

Heaven Above Fireworks is a company that turns your ashes into a firework after you die

Bullet proof vests, windshield wipers, fire escapes and laser printers were all invented by women

The Universe, the human brain and the Internet all have similar network structures

In 1994 Los Angeles Police arrested a man for dressing up as the Grim Reaper and standing outside the windows of old people

Charlie Chaplin is buried under six feet of concrete because his body was stolen in 1978

The Rock actually created the word "Smackdown"

From the late 1860s until the 1970s cities in the US had "ugly laws" which banned disabled people from appearing in public

Unicorns are mentioned in the bible

Sunlight hitting the earth right now was trapped inside the sun for 30,000 years before being released

23% of all photocopier faults are due to people photocopying their buttocks

25,000,000 cells died in your body while you read this sentence

95% of the universe is made of 'Dark Matter' and no one knows what dark matter is

In 2002 a garbage man won 19 million dollars, he spent it on gambling prostitutes and drugs and today he is back being a garbage man

Every year at least one person gets shot by a dog

Einstein's brain was stolen during his autopsy

The least successful Harry Potter movie earned 90 million more than the most successful Twilight movie

The word Oxymoron is an oxymoron, Oxy is Greek for sharp and moron means dull

America once used a five cent bill

Cockroaches feel the same way of us as we do about them, if you touch a cockroach it will run away, hide and then wash itself

Magician Harry Houdini actually died on Halloween

Dolly Parton once anonymously entered into a Dolly Parton look-a-like contest only to lose out to a drag queen

Harry Potter is the most banned book of the 21st Century

In 2001 Ashton Kutcher's girlfriend was murdered by a serial killer

The only member of the Beach Boys who actually surfed, drowned in 1983

There is a town in Newfoundland called Dildo

Engines in a Ferrari are musically engineered to sound perfect by utilizing the 3rd and 6th harmonics on the air intake, like and organ or flute

While inspecting fragments of Shakespeare's pipes researchers found traces of cannabis, cocaine and myristic acid

In comic books Spiderman grew up at 20 Ingram Street in Queens. That address exists in real life and the family that lives there is the Parkers

Every windmill on Earth turns counter-clockwise except in Ireland

If you inhale a pea it is possible for it to sprout and grow in your lungs

From 1784-1789 the US had a state called Franklin, today it is known as Tennessee

People born 1995-1999 have lived through 3 decades, 2 centuries and 2 millenniums

The final episode of the Tom and Jerry show ends with both of them committing suicide

A Chinese man once sued his wife for being too ugly and the Court agreed awarding him $115,000.00

Every year 86,000 people are injured by tripping over their pets

There is a 500 year old statue in Bern, Switzerland of a man eating a sack of babies, and no one knows why

Cheese is the most stolen food in the world

Betty White has been nominated for an Emmy in six different decades

Norwegians pay half the regular tax rate in November so people have more money at Christmas

In zoos, monkeys are given human birth control pills

People with ADD/ADHD have a better sense of smell

Most of the laugh tracks you hear on television were recorded in the 1950s, which means most of them are dead

The Harvard University Library collection actually has four books bound in human skin

In the original Italian story Pinocchio, Pinocchio kills Jiminy Cricket with a hammer

If you keep a goldfish in a dark room it will turn white

The earliest same sex wedding on record was performed in 65 A.D.

Che Guevara and Fidel Castro raised their national literacy rate from 60% to 90% in one year

Bob Barker (original host of the Price is Right) is a karate expert and trained with Chuck Norris for eight years

The British Army issues antimicrobial underwear that soldiers can wear for months at a time

Salema Porgy is a fish that causes hallucinations when consumed and was used as a recreational drug by the Roman Empire

Ryan Gosling was asked to audition to be a Back Street Boy but chose acting instead

A "butt load" is an actual measurement of volume, equal to 126 gallons

Peter the Great actually created The Council of Drunken Fools, a group whose sole job was to drink and party

The president of Uruguay is the poorest president in the world because he donates 90% of his salary to charity

The average millionaire goes bankrupt at least 3.5 times

Throughout the entire Twilight saga there are over 24 minutes of characters just staring at nothing

In Kansas if a woman rapes a man and gets pregnant she can sue the victim for child support

Dead people can still get goose bumps

Sleeping on the job is acceptable in Japan, it is seen as exhaustion from hard work and many people fake it to look more committed to their job

Freddie Mercury held parties where little people were hired to carry around trays of cocaine

Montreal has a musical swing set downtown, when in motion it creates sound, if you sync all 3 swings it creates a composition

"Killing season" is a British medical term used to describe a time, around August, when the newly qualified doctors join the NHS

The world's shortest horror story is two sentences long: The last man on earth sat alone in a room, there was a knock at the door

Scientists have found a way to connect the brains of two different people together and use one to control the body of the other

Jack Daniels ran away at 6 years old and learned to make whiskey from a Lutheran Minister

In 2001 a man from Minnesota was arrested for turning a vibrator into an explosive and giving it to his ex-girlfriend for Christmas.

Steve Irwin's last words before being pierced in the chest by a stingray were "don't worry they usually don't swim backwards"

In 2008 the remains of a woman Hedviga Golik was discovered. She had been sitting dead in front of her TV for 42 years

You get your billionth second of life when you are 31 years old

If an employee reports their company for tax evasion he or she will receive 30% of the amount collected by the US Government

Daniel Radcliffe purposely wore the same outfit for six months just to piss off the paparazzi making it look like the same old shot

"Never odd or even" spelled backwards is "never odd or even"

There are refrigerators full of beer scattered throughout Europe that can only be opened by scanning a Canadian passport

Steve Jobs refused to wear his oxygen mask while sick because he did not like the way it was designed

Just like humans, cows moo in accents specific to their region

In 1914 the first ever air-to-air combat included two planes, two pilots and two handguns and one of the planes was actually shot down

Every month that begins with a Sunday has a Friday the 13th

Dr Dre has made more money making headphones than he did making music

Prince Jefri Bolkiah of Brunei has blown through $14 Billion, spending more than any living person; he also has a super yacht that he named 'Tits'

The word slut was originally used to describe a woman who didn't keep her room clean

On average humans have anywhere from 2-5 pounds of bacteria inside their bodies

The German word for tramp stamp is "arschgeweih" which literally means ass antlers

There are more face book users today than there are books in the entire world

Sandwiches actually taste better when other people make them for you. When we make food we get desensitized to the smell

Until 1987 news broadcasters in the United States were legally required by the FCC to present both sides of whatever issue they were addressing

Hurricane Sandy sunk the ship used in "Pirates of the Caribbean"

The first webcam was used in 1991 by researchers at Cambridge who wanted to check the status of their coffee without leaving their desks

Ice worms live in glaciers, when exposed to temperatures above 40 degrees F they melt

Television actor Bryan Cranston was actually taught how to make meth by the DEA in preparation for his role in Breaking Bad

Every year a masked man leaves roses and cognac at Edgar Allen Poe's grave

The Catholic Church owns a media company that publishes pornography and erotica

There are stars in the Universe that are cold enough to be touched by the human hand

Blind people experience visual hallucinations when they take LSD

Since 2006, nickels and pennies have had a production cost greater than their face value, resulting in a taxpayer net loss of $436 million

Samhainophobia is the intense fear of Halloween

God is the only characters on the Simpsons to be drawn with five fingers on each hand

On record, there has never been a razorblade found in an apple

Many shelters do not allow black cats to be adopted on Halloween for fear that they might be tortured or sacrificed

Will Smith, Dan Rather and Vanilla Ice all were born on Halloween

An 18 year old once tried to eat his underwear in hopes that the cotton fabric would absorb alcohol before he took a breathalyzer test

The abbreviation LOL is sometimes used by librarians for little old ladies

In 1954 a man committed suicide by jumping off the golden gate bridge. His suicide note said "no reason, except I have a toothache"

The dildo was invented 15,000 years before the wheel

Jim Carrey would write Tupac funny letters while he was in prison to help make him smile

In the comic strip, Casper the Friendly Ghost was a teenager who died of pneumonia after sledding all day

Every year the Netherlands sends 20,000 tulips to Canada as thanks for all the aid they provided during WWII

In 1963 Stephen Hawking was told he only had two years to live.

The US has 115,000 Janitors, 83,000 bartenders, 323,000 restaurant servers, and 80,000 heavy-duty truck drivers with Bachelor's degrees

"Snow White" and "King Kong" were Adolf Hitler's two favorite movies

A man named Joseph Bolitho Johns escaped Australian prison so many times they built a special cell just for him, he escaped that as well

When you fall asleep, the colder a room is, the greater the chances for a nightmare

Before writing children books Dr. Seuss wrote adult books such as "Boners" and "More Boners"

The mating ritual of a sloth including foreplay takes place and finishes within five seconds

In 2016, a Florida man was fined $48,000.00 by the Federal Communications Commission for using a cell phone signal jammer during his commute, he wanted to keep other drivers from using their phones while driving

Salvador Dali would avoid paying tabs by drawing on the checks. The drawings would be too valuable to cash the check

Squirrels and elephants purr like kittens

The Nazis invented exploding chocolate bars. These were uncovered by British intelligence during WWII, but they were never used

When Montenegro became independent from Yugoslavia its internet domain name went from .yu to .me

In a Disney comic called "Mickey Mouse and the Medicine Man". Goofy and Mickey become drug dealers

In 2010 there was a major traffic jam in China that lasted for about 12 days

Leo Fender, creator of Fender Guitars, never knew how to play guitar

Women in ancient Rome wore the sweat of Gladiators to improve their beauty and complexion

Wealthy parents have been known to hire handicapped children to go to Disney World with them so they can skip the lines

British spies would use semen as invisible ink during WWII, this was discovered by a man named Mansfield Cumming

Smoking near Apple computers voids the warranty

70% of Raccoons carry a parasite that can consume your brains and eyeballs

According to the Bible, Satan's number is actually 616 not 666

In the city of La Paz, Bolivia there is a bar called Route 36. It is the world's first cocaine serving bar

Queen Elizabeth served as a mechanic and driver during WWII

Crepitus was the Roman God of flatulence

When you pee a small amount of urine enters your mouth through the saliva glands

Beethoven was once arrested for looking like a tramp

The price of entry into a zoo in the 18th century England was a dog
or a cat; they were fed to the lions

The word "nerd" was actually invented by Dr. Seuss

Illinois in 2008 a woman had to have her dachshund called Roscoe
put down after the dog gnawed off her big toe while she slept

The French often use the expression "the English have landed" to
say a woman is on her period

A single strand of spaghetti is called spaghetto

The witness protection program in the US has never had a breach
of security in which a protected person or family members was
harmed

Hitler was said to have used meth in order to treat his Parkinson's
disease

Luis Garavito, the world's most dangerous serial killer (140 victims)
only has to serve 22 more years in prison and should be released in
2021

In 1995 a man stole a tank in Southern California and drove it down
a freeway

Bees and wasps can be trained like dogs to detect explosives and
drugs

Ancient Romans would use a sponge on a stick instead of toilet
paper

Adolf Hitler's nephew, William fought for the US against his uncle in
WWII

When it was first created, the internet was known as the galactic
network

Every Chili's restaurant has one picture hanging upside-down inside
and it's a challenge for the customers to find it

Thanksgiving dinner at the white house in 1909 included a turkey, a 50 pound mince pie and a 26 pound possum said to be the largest and plumpest ever trapped in the Georgia woods

There is a bar in Ireland that opened in 900 AD and is still operational. It's named "Sean's bar"

Queen is the only group in which every member of the group has composed more than one number 1 single

It takes 364 licks to get to the tootsie roll center of a tootsie pop

Rick Moranis was on board to do a Spaceballs sequel called: Spaceballs III: The search for Spaceballs II

According to Discovery Magazine scientists have recently discovered certain brain parasites that can facilitate a zombie apocalypse

Costco hasn't changed the price of its $1.50 hot dog/soda combo since 1985

The most successful pirate captain was actually a Chinese prostitute; she had 80,000 sailors working for her

Rich people in Russia often hire fake ambulances to beat city traffic, inside is not medical equipment but sofas and a flat screen TV

In the 1980s Mike Tyson caught his wife in bed with Brad Pitt

In 1962 the US Government planned terrorist attacks on US cities they called Operation Northwoods, they wanted to blame Cuba so they could start a war

Ants nod to one another as they pass by each other

A pack of man-eating wolves ate 40 people in Paris in 1450 before finally being defeated by citizens on the steps of Notre Dame

During WWII, Japan bombed China with fleas that had been infected with the bubonic plague

Fruit flies tend to drink alcohol after being rejected as a mate

A hammerhead shark can be rendered completely immobile for 15 minutes by turning it over and tickling its tummy

56 million years ago horses the size of ducks roamed North America

Pandas do not have a specific spot to sleep in; they sleep wherever they happen to be

Mosquitoes have killed more humans than all wars in history

Elephants have been known to rescue other animals, such as trapped dogs

Cows give more milk while listening to music

In 1859 Australians released 24 rabbits within six years the population grew to 2 million

Koalas have fingerprints nearly identical to the fingerprints of humans

Elephants have been known to rape and kill grown rhinos

Sea otters have been known to rape and drown baby seals

Right now there is a bacterium in your eye that is pooping and mating

Whenever a hurricane/large storm approaches the US, beer and Pop-tarts become the most purchased items at Wal-Mart

Scientists recently discovered a 3,500 year old tablet containing what is believed to be the world's oldest "yo mamma" joke

Portugal decriminalized all drugs eleven years ago and the number of drug addicts in the country decreased 50%

Thomas Jefferson hated banks and stated that they were "more dangerous than armies"

Dinosaurs lived on planet Earth for 150 million years, humans have lived on the planet for just .01% of that time

Kryptonite was invented because Superman's original voice actor wanted time off and the only way to do it was to make Superman sick

Female squid can wear fake testicles to avoid advancements from men

France is the only European country that is completely self-sufficient in basic food production

Coca-Cola made a fruit-flavored soda for the Nazis when there was a syrup shortage – and that is how Fanta was created

Ronald Wayne co-founder of Apple sold his 10% share in 1976 for $2,300.00. Today it's worth over 58 billion

Due to the high amount of granite in its construction, Grand Central Station now produces more radiation than is permitted at a Nuclear Plant

Since 1949 every treasurer of the United States has been a woman

8% of the worlds currency is physical money, the rest only exists on computers

In the city of Beijing, Inhaling the air is equal to smoking 21 cigarettes a day

You can buy Gourmet Clam Chowder flavored Doritos in Japan

The British won a battle in Jerusalem by giving the enemy large amounts of Opium and getting them high

At any time, about .07% of the world is drunk, so roughly 50 million people are drunk right now

Iraq and Afghanistan have universal healthcare that's provided by funding from the US

In 2002 Bruce Willis purchased 12,000 boxes of Girl Scout cookies for American troops that were stationed throughout the Middle East

"Morning after" pills don't work for women who weigh over 176 pounds

When you look up and see little white dots you're actually seeing your own white blood cells

Originally, the song "Here comes the Bride" was part of an Opera about mass murder

Nearly 60% of terrorists graduated school with degrees in engineering

Time moves a bit faster 12 inches above the ground as opposed to at ground level – This means your feet are slightly younger than your head

Residents in South Africa can legally attach flamethrowers to the sides of their cars to repel carjackers

It took 200,000 years for the human population to reach 3 billion – it only took 40 years for it to grow by another 3 billion after that

After Germany surrendered in WWII, people in Moscow partied until the entire city actually ran out of vodka

A 27 year old mother once called the cops on her son for opening his Christmas presents early to teach him a lesson

The strings attached to boxes of animal crackers were originally put there so the box could be hung on a Christmas tree

William Whipple freed all of his slaves after signing the Declaration of Independence – He felt he could not fight for freedom and own slaves at the same time

The first text message was sent on December 3, 1992 it said "merry Christmas"

The Swine flu outbreak in 1976 killed one person but the vaccine for the Swine Flu killed 25

Every year in New York City 1,600 people are bitten by other humans

A Chicago High School once played Justin Beiber's song "Baby" between classes and students had to pay to stop it. They earned $1,000.00 in three days

Some holocaust survivors died of chocolate and candy overdoses within their first week of freedom

France has the best European military, in 800 years they have fought in 185 battles and won 132 of them

In 1994 a woman named Lucy Moro was found guilty of manslaughter after kicking her husband in the balls and accidentally killed him

Canadian Police once found a marijuana plantation that was guarded by 13 black bears

The Nintendo, Wii, Playstation, and Xbox are all banned in China even though they are all manufactured in China

Russia and Japan never signed a peace treaty ending WWII

Kobe Bryant's middle name is Bean

A woman once farted on an airplane and tried to cover it up by lighting matches – She caused an emergency landing

In 1965 a 9 year old boy nearly drowned at a local beach but was rescued by a woman named Alice Blaise. Nine years later that same boy (now a teenager) at that same beach saved a drowning man that turned out to be Alice's husband

Captain Morgan was a real person. He was a Welsh pirate who later became the Lieutenant Governor of Jamaica

One of the first people to legally own a slave in the American Colonies was a black man named Anthony Johnson

Ants bury other ants after they die

Medieval Japanese Samurai would burn incense in their helmets so if they were decapitated their heads would smell good

A grown man once hunted down and attacked a child who killed him in the video game Call of Duty

In the 1980s video gamers could photograph their television screen showing a high score and mail it to the company Activision, who would in turn send back a patch

Wombat poop is cube shaped

Samuel L. Jackson had the phrase "Bad Motherf#cker" engraved on the light saber he used in the Star Wars films

The Earth's helium supply will run out in 2030 and party balloons will cost about $90.00

Every pound of fat you gain causes the body to generate seven miles of blood vessels

There is an unknown object in the nearby galaxy M82 that started sending out radio waves. The emission looks like nothing we have ever seen before

Mexico's 34th president ruled for less than one hour and then quit

Bubble wrap was originally intended to be used as wallpaper

A man once tried to blow up the Eiffel Tower because its light was shinning into his bedroom window keeping him up at night

The first recorded use of "OMG" was in a letter to Winston Churchill written in 1917

The lowest musical note in the known universe is caused by the rumbling of a black hole in the Perseus galaxy that is 57 octaves below middle C

In movie theaters throughout the United States, popcorn costs more per ounce than filet mignon

One of the first scientists to discover Nitrous Oxide completely missed its use as an anesthetic because he only used it to get himself high

First Lady Eleanor Roosevelt would only allow female journalists at her press conferences ensuring that the newspapers would hire woman journalists

The US is the serial killer capital of the world

Ecstasy was named and made popular by Catholic Priest Michael Clegg. It was made illegal after he tried to bring it to the masses

Worms communicate by snuggling

In 1524 a statue of the Virgin Mary was found guilty of being a witch and was burned

In a 2004 song Cookie Monster revealed that his name is Sid

Black Friday has a different meaning to those living in Australia, it refers to a series of brushfires that wiped out entire towns and killed 71 people

In the 1970s Captain Crunch cereal came with a toy that could be modified to hack telephone lines

A chicken named Mike lived for a year and a half without his head

The Humpty Dumpty rhyme never states that he is an egg

The last murder to happen in the country Liechtenstein was in 2007

Humans are the only mammals that can't swallow and breathe at the same time

A woodchuck can chuck about 136 cubic centimeters of wood

Chicken today contains 266% more fat and 33% less protein than it did 40 years ago

President Gerald Ford held a high school prom at the White House for his daughter

Martha Stewart's prison name was M. Diddy

The reason Pirates wore eye patches is to have one eye adjusted for the sunny top deck and the other already adjusted for the darkness when going below deck.

Peanut butter was originally sold in slices, like cheese

Pokémon holds the record for most photosensitive epileptic seizures caused by a TV show

Between 1912 and 1948 art competitions were part of the Olympics. Medals were awarded for architecture, music, painting and sculpture

In ancient Greece the word "idiot" meant anyone who wasn't a politician

A woman once sued Nickelodeon claiming it was their fault she couldn't have sex

There is a population of radioactive wild boars in Germany, caused by the Chernobyl disaster two decades ago, and their numbers are rising

The Grammy Awards were invented to counter the exploding popularity of Rock 'n Roll in the 1950s

Islendingabok is an app that helps prevent Icelanders from having sex with their relatives (which happens often)

We lose six seconds of visual information every minute from blinking – so during a 150 minute movie, our eyes are shut for about 15 minutes

Bob Marley's father was actually a white man from England

Contrary to popular belief, carrots are actually bad for rabbits

Lack of crime has forced the Netherlands to close eight prisons across their country

In 2005 a man named Ronald MacDonald robbed a Wendy's

In 1942 there was a man called the Phantom Barber. He would break into peoples' houses in Mississippi at night and cut their hair

For $295.00 you can get an exorcism over Skype

Saddam Hussein and George W. Bush both had their shoes hand-made by the same Italian shoemaker

In 2003 Dave Grohl was on the top of the Billboard Rock Charts as a member of three different bands for 17 weeks in a row

Ernest Hemingway and Benjamin Franklin both enjoyed writing in the nude

10% of United States electricity is made from dismantled nuclear bombs

On the day of Alexander Graham Bell was buried, the entire United States telephone system was shut down for one minute in tribute

The Co-creator of Tetris brutally murdered his family because he never received any money from the games success

Costa Rica abolished its military and now spends the money on education and culture

The ear of the Asian elephant is shaped like India where as the ear of the African elephant is shaped like Africa

While on his deathbed Voltaire was asked by priests to renounce the devil. His sarcastic reply was "this is no time to start making new enemies"

The oldest surviving love poem to date is written on a clay tablet from the times of Sumerians (the inventors of writing) around 3,500 B.C.

Men who grow beards easily and earlier in life are more likely to go bald

Prior to violence in video games, parents were blaming "Dungeons and Dragons" for teen Satanism and suicide

There is a hidden room behind Lincoln's head on Mount Rushmore

British Intelligence once hacked into an Al-Qaeda website and replaced instructions on how to make a bomb with a cup cake recipe

In the middle ages, young men and women would draw names from a bowl to see who their Valentine was. For one week they pinned the name on their sleeves for everyone to see. This is the origin of the phrase "wear ones heart on their sleeve."

Sloths poop only once a week

Alexander Graham Bell applied for his patent on the telephone on Valentine's Day, 1876

Joker-Toxin is real; it comes from the poisonous Hemlock water-droplet plant that leaves the victim with a smile on their face at the time of death

The first female self-made millionaire in America was a black woman

The creators of Adidas and Puma were brothers; in addition they were both Nazis

Stairs kill 12,000 people per year; elevators kill about 27 per year

At least 5 people have reportedly been murdered for unfriending someone on Face book

Freud liked cocaine so much that he would give it to his family and friends as gifts

The word "scumbag" was originally used to refer to a used condom

Boobytrap spelled backwards is "party boob"

The cigarette lighter was invented before the match

The North and South Korean armies choose their physically toughest looking soldiers to have "stare downs" across the Korean border

800 different languages are spoken in New York City

Approximately 250 dead people are currently frozen and waiting to be revived with future technology

Only female mosquitoes bite, the male ones are vegetarians

Marlin and Dory would have to swim 1,568 miles to find Nemo

The world's first Buddhist ruler Emperor Ashoka was the first ruler in human history to ban slavery, animal cruelty and deforestation

One American consumes the same amount of resources as 32 Kenyans

George Takei once called for peace between Star Trek fans and Star Wars fans and unite against Twilight fans

When dragonflies mate their tails form a heart

The North Star is actually a handful of stars orbiting around each other

Scientists have created bullet proof armor out of a liquid that hardens upon contact

In Ireland it was tradition that if you donated a pint of blood, you would receive a pint of Guinness to replace the lost iron

The Lion King is the highest grossing hand drawn film in history

Cats bite over 40,000 Americans each year and have hunted 33 species into extinction

In 2008, McDonalds saved $278,850,000.00 by removing one of the two slices of cheese from the McDouble Cheeseburger

Mahatma Gandhi used to travel with his goat so that he could always have fresh milk

At least three people who have been on Gordon Ramsay's cooking shows have gone on to commit suicide

Before trees became common, the world was covered in giant mushrooms

World War 1 killed twice as many cows as it did humans

Mozart composed a song titled "leck mir den Arsch fein recht schon sauber" which means "lick my ass right, well and clean"

After drinking 3 bottles of Vodka, a Russian man jumped out of a five story window, walked back up, and jumped again

Paper can only be recycled six times, after the filters become too weak to hold anything together

Dung beetles are the only insects that can navigate the earth by the position of the Milky Way Galaxy and bright stars

Picasso burned most of his early work to keep his apartment warm because he was poor

Eddie Van Halen didn't ask for royalties after completing Michael Jackson's "Beat It" guitar solo, he did it as a favor

Grizzly bears can run faster than horses and can maintain the speed indefinitely

Of the Catholic Church's list of banned books Les Miserables is one of them

In 2009 Coolio attempted to stage dive during a performance. Nobody caught him, he was beaten up and had his shoes stolen

In 1914 a Dorset poultry farmer published an article stating that he has achieved remarkable growth rates by electrifying his chickens

Naked means unprotected, nude means unclothed

Since 1997 the company Monsanto has had one lawsuit filed against it every three weeks for sixteen years and Monsanto won every case

Usain Bolt ate nothing but chicken nuggets while competing in Beijing because that was the only thing he knew. He won three gold medals

Ghengis Khan killed 11% of the world's population

Marijuana was initially made illegal in 1937 by a man who testified the drug made white women want to be with black men

A 555 pound woman lost 443 pounds in one year by eating nothing but baby food

There is an abandoned island at Disney World called 'Discovery Island', once three guys swam out to it and found snakes preserved in coke bottles

Dog the Bounty Hunter once bailed Nicolas Cage out of Jail

Air Jordans were banned by the NBA; however Michael Jordan always wore them as Nike was willing to pay the fine for each game

80% of the world's natural forests have been destroyed

A fifteen minute film of Marilyn Monroe engaging in oral sex was purchased by a New York business man for $1.5 million

Gordon Ramsey had to leave his first job as a chef because he had an affair with his owner's wife

The most expensive coffee in the world is harvested from civet poop

In 2004 three independent studies all reported massively high amounts of Methane within the atmosphere of Mars. On Earth, all methane is created by living organisms

There is a Giant Hornet from Japan that is four inches long but its venom will dissolve human skin

There is a Declaration of Galactic Independence as well as the Constitution of the Galactic Government which sets rules for outer space

The average Canadian is richer than the average American

Pigasus was a pig who ran for president of the United States in 1968

Coming up with a solution that actually makes the problem worse is called the 'Cobra Effect'

The sign language equivalent to tongue twisters is known as 'finger fumblers'

Prince Eric from the "Little Mermaid" is the only Disney prince who does not sing in a Disney film

Chickens with white earlobes will lay white eggs, while chickens with red earlobes will lay brown eggs

In Asia today there are more tigers living as pets then there are living in the wild

Japanese electronics company Panasonic announced recently that its workers in China will now receive compensation for living with hazardous air pollution

In Finland, the cost of a speeding ticket is determined by the driver's annual income

Pope Francis has a Masters Degree in Chemistry

Dead people can still have orgasms

The Carrington Event occurred in 1859, it was a giant solar storm that hit planet Earth. During the event telegraph machines continued to send/receive messages despite being disconnected from its power source and several operators reported electric shocks from the machines

Billionaire Chuck Feeney gave away 99% of his 6.3 billion to help underprivileged kids go to college, he is now worth 2 million

In Dubai, the police fleet includes a Ferrari, Lamborghini and Bentley, that way they can catch speeders that would be able to outrun other police vehicles

J.K. Rowling wrote the final chapter of the 7th Harry Potter book 9 years before the 1st book was even released

Mexico has the highest average annual hours worked in the world

Stray dogs in Moscow have learned to use the city's subway system, in the morning they ride the subway to downtown where they scavenge and beg for food and at the end of the day they get back on the subway and go home, getting off at their required stops

In the 1960s CIA field agents would occasionally prank each other by slipping each other LSD

Octopi make undersea gardens by collecting stones/shiny things and arranging them in the sand

In the Bible, God sent two bears to murder 42 children because they mocked a bald man

When polar bears are angry they hiss like cats

July 23, 2012 two blasts of super-hot plasma was ejected from the sun at the same time, they slammed into one another forming the most powerful solar eruption in the history of the space age. If our planet had been in its path it would have been a life altering event

The founder of FED EX, Fred Smith once saved the company by taking $5,000.00 to Las Vegas and turning it onto $32,000.00 by playing Black Jack

Ice-T released a song titled "99 problems" eleven years before Jay-Z did, with the same chorus

A "cunt hair" is the second smallest unit of measurement, used for nearly infinitesimal distances

Every year, since 1999, Girl Scout Cookies bring in about $700 million in revenue

More than 900 workers have already died preparing for the 2022 World Cup in Qatar

When you get "blackout drunk" you don't really forget anything because your brain never tried remembering those events in the first place

Squirrels forget where they hide about half of the nuts they collect and thanks to that hundreds of new trees grow every year

There is a nuclear bomb somewhere lost off the coast of Georgia

Cats can make over 100 different sounds; dogs can only make around 10 different sounds

Indoor tanning has caused more cases of skin cancer then smoking has caused cases of lung cancer

The opposite of ambidextrous is ambisinister and it means you are equally clumsy with both hands

Flushing your toilet actually sends fecal matter and other bacteria into the air flying around your bathroom, it's better to flush the toilet with the lid down

Bees normally buzz in the key of A, but when they are tired, they buzz in the key of E

Astronauts grew a rose in space just to see if it would smell different…. And it did

The Ancient Romans used to use a plant called Silphium as a contraceptive; the Romans drove the plant into extinction.

In 2010 a Canadian man rescued a newborn baby from a dumpster, only to find out he was the father

Lil Wayne accidentally shot himself in the chest at age 12

Ladybugs are named after the Virgin Mary; they are extremely promiscuous and have the highest rates of STDs among insects

The word for fox in Norwegian is also slang for marijuana, which was a bit of inspiration behind the song "what does the fox say"

Bob Marley's last words to his son Ziggy were "money can't buy life"

Stephen King was once hit by a van. He ended up buying the van and destroyed it to make himself feel better

90% of the world's data has been created in the last two years

Jehovah's Witness don't celebrate birthdays because the only two accounts of birthday parties in the Bible ended in murder

During the middle ages talkative women were punished by being forced to wear metal cages on their heads

CEOs are more likely to be psychopaths than any other profession

It snows metal on the planet Venus

In France a bakery is required by law to make all of its bread it sells from scratch in order to have the right to be called a bakery

The word mortgage comes from a French word that means "pledge to death"

The pyramids were as old to the Romans as the Romans are to us

A tortoise named "Adwaita" lived to be 255 years old. He was born before the United States existed and his death was announced on CNN (1750-2006)

If you pronounce the names of products wrong while in an Apple store, the employees are not allowed to correct you

Humans are bioluminescent, but the light emitted by the body is 1,000 times weaker than what our eyes can register

Socrates taught Plato, Plato taught Aristotle, Aristotle taught Alexander the Great

The inventor of Petroleum Jelly ate a spoonful of it every day claiming it had great health benefits. He lived to be 96

A dragonfly has a lifespan of 24 hours

The South Korean government demands that big retail giants like Tesco and Costco be closed two Sundays a month to support small businesses

All clams are born male and some change to female later in life, they cannot change back

The North American Lottery system makes more than the movie, music and porn industry combined

Bob Marley gave the credit for "No woman, no cry" to a friend who ran a soup kitchen to ensure the royalty checks would keep it open

The ashes of the man that discovered Pluto are on their way to the planet as you read this

There is an international zip line between Spain and Portugal

In the original version of Sleeping Beauty, she was raped by the King and gave birth to 2 children, all before she woke up

A boy weighing 6lb 6oz was born during the 6th hour of 06/06/06, his name is Damien

UPS trucks collectively save 10 million gallons of gas every year because they avoid left turns as much as possible

Alisha Halfmoon, a woman from Tulsa Oklahoma, once spent six hours inside a Wal-Mart building a meth lab

The longest human poop ever recorded was 26 feet long

Jim Carrey used to write Tupac funny letters to help him smile and laugh while he was in prison

In that 70s Show, the character 'Fes' name means Foreign Exchange Student

A man's beard grows faster when he is anticipating sex

There are 4 people living in the US with the name "Fuk Yu"

The runtime of the movie Titanic is the same amount of time it took for the ship to sink; 3 hours 14minutes

The Island of Manhattan was purchased from the Algonquin Indians in 1624 for $24.00

Actually MTV's show "16 and Pregnant" has been linked to a decrease in teen pregnancies

A Mexican man who accidentally killed his cousin while drunk was sentenced to death by being buried alive next to the cousin he had killed

There are approximately 7,184 people in the world just like you

The Beatles would refuse to play at American concerts where audiences were segregated and wrote that into their contracts

Mike Duke, the CEO of Wal-Mart, makes more in an hour than his employees do in a year

"Muggle" was a slang term used for marijuana mainly among the jazz community in the 1920s and 1930s

Seven people died by drowning in 300.000 gallons of spilled beer during the London Beer Flood of 1814

Pepto-Bismol turns into chunks of metal when lit with a blowtorch

Samuel L. Jackson is the highest grossing actor of all time

There are special roads in Japan that make music when you drive over them

The probability of you drinking a glass of water that contains a molecule of water that passed through a dinosaur is almost 100%

Turtles can breathe out of their butts

The band Creed once put on such a bad show that a $1,800,000.00 class action lawsuit was filed on behalf of all the fans in attendance

One billion teenagers are entering their reproductive years; this is the largest "Youth quake" ever

Betty White is older than sliced bread

In addition to love, St. Valentine is also the patron saint of plagues

Workers at various IPad factories operate in conditions so horrible, they are forced to sign anti-suicide pledges

Despite the many references to Germany in the movie "Django Unchained" (which was set in 1858), Germany didn't exist until 1871

"Gold Pills" are sold at $425.00 each. When consumed they will turn your poop into glittering gold

In Malaysia, it is legal to divorce your partner via text message

The people of Buganda, who live in Uganda, speak Luganda

Pink Floyd's dark side of the moon spent 741 weeks on the Billboard charts from 1973 to 1988, longer than any other album in history

A whale's vomit is worth about $5,000 a pound

The Horror Frog will break his/her own bones to make claws out of them and use them as defensive weapons

12 men have stepped onto the moon but only 3 have been to the deepest part of our oceans

According to the real Mayan Calendar the actual date of the apocalypse is October 13, 4772

Scientists are working on tattoos that can make electronic telekinesis possible

Martin Luther King Jr., Anne Frank and Barbara Walters were all born on the same year (1929)

Oxford University is older than the Aztec Empire

 A Russian woman died of a heart attack after waking up and realizing she was at her own funeral

Prescription drugs kill more people each year than heroin and cocaine combined

Drug lord Pablo Escobar had so much cash that rats ate nearly $1 billion of his money each year

World population growth is equivalent to around 3 babies per second

A recent study concluded that parents tend to put their "cuter" children's safety and happiness before their "uglier" children

Prior to 1940s pink was a masculine color; preferred by men while blue was more of a feminine color

You can electronically shock a person's brain to greatly improve their math skills for up to six months

If his father did not change his name, Hitler's name would have been "Adolf Schicklgruber"

An inmate named Joseph Dekenipp escaped a detention center in Arizona on Valentine's Day just to spend some time with his girlfriend

Joseph Stalin said at his wife's funeral "this creature softened my heart of stone, with her death goes my last warm feelings toward humanity"

The companies Hugo Boss, Siemes, IBM, Bayers, and Volkswagen all worked with the Nazis

Willie Nelson once smoked weed on the roof of the White House

On April 1, 2007, (April fool's Day) Google sent out an email to its employees saying a python was loose in their office, they weren't kidding

The earliest recorded uses of marijuana dates back to the 3rd millennium BC

Spazzstick is a brand of Chapstick that's made with caffeine to keep you alert

In New York City the Polar Vortex was so harsh that it drove the rats to eat trees just to survive

Out of 28 states that have banned texting while driving, 22 of them offer traffic updates via twitter

All the stars in the sky outnumber every sound and word produced by every human that has ever lived

Vision is the quickest sense we have; our sense of smell is the most delayed

A squids' brain is doughnut shaped and their esophagus runs through it; if a squid eats something too big it can result in severe brain damage

You can live for weeks without eating but will most likely die 11 days without sleep

Saddam Hussein's 2002 campaign song was an Arabic version of Whitney Houston's song "I will always love you"

A 10 year old boy in England once underwent emergency medical treatment to have his testicle reattached after a wedgie

Farts travel an average speed of 10 feet per second

Cleopatra's last name was Ptolemy and she was Greek, not Egyptian

You can now text 911 in case of an emergency

In 2008 social media overtook porn as the number one online activity

Ellen DeGeneres was originally offered the part of Phoebe in "Friends" but she turned it down

In the original version of the fairy tale Cinderella actually kills her stepmother first so that her father could marry their housekeeper

Only 8% of the world's currency exists as physical cash, the rest is electronic

Litter from modern civilization has become so pervasive that scientists conducting the first ever study of undersea trash could not find any place (including some of the deepest oceans) where trash did not exist

Mosquitoes don't just bite you. They urinate on you after sucking your blood

In 2011, a man was stabbed to death by a rooster

Albert Einstein never wore socks

923 words break the "I before e" rule; only 44 words actually follow the rule

Abraham Lincoln's grandfather was also named Abraham Lincoln. He was shot and killed as well

Every 3 days new inhabitants to this planet add the equivalent of a city the size of San Francisco to world population numbers

Humans shed and grow a new outer layer of skin every 27 days

As a child, Jim Carrey wore tap shoes in bed just in case his parents needed a little laughter in the middle of the night

Chocolate milk was invented in Ireland

The record for the longest amount of time between the births of twins is 87 days

Sylvester Graham invented the Graham cracker under the impression that the taste would stop people from masturbating

From the 1500s to the 1800s the word 'occupy' referred to sexual relations

The shredded "cheddar cheese" on Taco Bell tacos does not melt when put to fire, it burns.

Terry Fox was a 21 year old, one-legged cancer patient who ran 3339 miles across Canada in 143 days before dying

A ship sank in Alaskan waters during the gold rush and as much as $260 million in gold has yet to be discovered

In Switzerland you can rent fake police cars to park at your house so burglars stay away

Crabs have blue blood, while leeches and worms have green blood

Singapore Airlines have 'corpse cupboards' to store people who die mid-flight

Torbernite is a real mineral that acts like kryptonite for humans. The closer you are, the weaker you become

Elsa (from the Disney film Frozen) is only the second Disney princess that was crowned Queen, Tiana from the Princess and the Frog was the other

In Peru it is tradition to give your friends and family yellow underpants on New Year's Eve

If the history of the entire earth was compressed into a single day, humans would have appeared at 11:58PM

In WWII the Russians trained dogs to run under German tanks with bombs strapped to their backs

The slang term "kiss my ass" dates as far back as the year 1705

Saliva can act as a painkiller that is 6 times more powerful than morphine

Nicolas Cage got paid 20 million dollars for playing the role of Superman… even though he never actually did

The actors who played C-3PO and R2-D2 hate each other in real life

The creator of Pringles had his ashes stored in a Pringles can after he died

Yo-Yos were originally developed for hunting

Humans are the slowest growing of all mammals

Plants can selectively abort seed embryos

Blood donors in Sweden are sent text messages every time their blood is used to save a life

Herrings communicate with each other by farting

The Nazi's had jet packs to launch Nazi soldiers over rivers and minefields

Scientists in Australia tagged a nine foot great white shark as part of a program that tracked these animals. Data from the tag shows the nine foot shark was abruptly dragged down into a deep ocean trench, then eaten

You can lead a cow upstairs but not downstairs, their knees can't bend properly to walk downstairs

Humans have more brain cells at the age of two than at any other time in their lives

The US Government search for Titanic was actually a cover up mission. The US was really looking for two lost nuclear submarines from the 1960s

Japan makes whale bacon

A man named Robert Vick once broke out of prison, then turned himself in because it was too cold outside

An 11 year old boy named Moshe Peer survived the gas chambers during WWII on six separate occasions

Koalas, chimps, gorillas and humans are the only animals that have fingerprints

When asked what would happen if he were invited to a dinner party with his characters Dr. Seuss said "I wouldn't show up"

Ants stretch and yawn when they wake up in the morning

"Bohemian Rhapsody" and "Hey Jude" were recorded using the same piano

The Chinese government censored the word "censored"

Just before his death, Nikola Tesla claimed he had perfected a "death beam"

Kamilo Beach, located on Hawaii's Big Island, is one of the dirtiest beaches in the world and It recently became the discovery site of a new formation: a rock made of plastic, sediment, lava, and organic debris.

Thursday is named after Thor the God of Thunder

Burt of "Burt's Bees" is real; He is 79 years old and lives in rural Maine

Ancient Greeks would not eat beans because they believed beans contained the souls of the dead

Steve Jobs was the executive producer for "Toy Story"

Ghengis Khan killed about 11% of the entire world's population

Dolphins have been known to go on killing sprees when sexually frustrated

The average lifespan of an eye lash is 150 days

In 1978 a US Navy ship was attacked by an unknown species of giant squid

In 1993, soccer fans in Bolivia accidentally burned down their entire village while celebrating their teams' win with fireworks

A man once wore 70 items of clothing in a Chinese airport to avoid the bagging charge

In England you are legally required to stop your car if you run over a dog, but not a cat

In 1970 the US Army secretly dumped 64 million pounds of nerve agents into the ocean, along with 400,000 bombs, land mines and rockets

When you crumple up gift wrapping, it forms a shape so complex that it will defeat even the most sophisticated of computers

Thirty five percent of people who use personal ads are already married

In 2002, Saudi Arabian police forced school girls to stay inside a burning building because they were not covered properly

A man once used his tractor to crush eight police cars because he was mad over a marijuana arrest

Some African prostitutes have developed immunity to HIV

Saturn's rings seem to disappear about every fourteen years

Most German men have been taught that standing up to pee is unhygienic and they sit to pee

Hitler's plan for Moscow was to kill all of its residents and cover it with an artificial lake

The word "junkie" originated from the 1920s when drug addicts would steal scrap metal to fund their addiction

EBay sees over one billion transactions per day

Ninth graders did an experiment and found that plants will not grow near Wi-Fi routers

Dartmouth College serves green eggs and ham to 90% of incoming freshmen in honor of Dr. Seuss

Mosquitoes prefer biting people who are drunk

330 million different gods are worshipped by the Hindu religion

The first ingredient listed on a box of goldfish crackers is "smiles"

In Denmark, you are required to check underneath your car for sleeping children before starting your car

Every 8 seconds a child dies from contaminated water

In a lifetime the average person will walk the equivalent of 5 times around the equator

When your face blushes, the lining of your stomach turns red as well

In the mid 1980s Fergie of the Black Eyed Peas was the voice of Charlie Brown's sister Sally

Abraham Lincoln was the first cat owner to become president of the United States

If you commit any crime at sea, you are considered a pirate

Wearing headphones for one hour will increase the bacteria in your ear 700 times

The CEO of American Apparel was forced to quit after dancing naked with two female employees in his office

Ancient Japanese poets would engage in rap battle sessions that displayed their skill and wit

Besides humans, elephants are the only animals that can be taught to stand on their head

A praying mantis only has one ear

Hawaiian Punch was originally developed in 1934 as a tropical flavored ice cream topping

A "moment" technically means 90 seconds

Any given microwave uses more electricity to power the clock than it does to heat your food

The owner of the company that makes Segways died in 2010 after driving his Segway off a cliff

At age 15, Jim Carrey quit school and became a janitor to support his family who at the time were living out of a van

The starfish is the only animal that can turn its stomach inside out

Lip balms dry out your lips, making you want more lip balm

Researchers have taken the HIV virus, modified it and then used it to reprogram a cancer patient's white blood cells to attack and completely kill off the cancer

All thirteen minerals required to sustain human life can be found in alcoholic beverages

"Almost" is the longest word in the English language with all of its letters in alphabetical order

Before the invention of the light bulb, people slept an average of 10 hours every night

Russians use the word "Zapoi" to describe several days of continuous drunkenness during which one withdraws from society

Diarrhea has killed more people in the 20th century than all the wars combined

In 1962 Bruce Lee landed 15 punches and a kick that knocked out his opponent in a fight which lasted 11 seconds

The Aztecs killed about 20,000 people every year to please their gods

Surgery patients heal faster when their room has a view of trees

Nipple make up is popular in Japan where you can change your nipple color according to your mood

People graduating college today have never been alive while the Simpsons wasn't on TV

A man once jumped from a 10-story window to commit suicide. On his way down, a stray bullet killed him instantly

The word "electrocute" is only accurate if the person dies

An Austrian man died of starvation while his wife was hospitalized because he refused to eat unless she prepared his food

It is believed King Edward II of England was murdered by having a red hot iron inserted into his anus

Helium is the only element that was discovered in space before it was found on earth

Americans throw away 25,000,000,000 Styrofoam coffee cups every year

The co-creator of Tetris brutally murdered his family because he never received any money from the game's success

Giraffes can't yawn

New studies show that people may unsuspectingly choose friends who have more DNA sequences in common

Scientists have discovered a giant cloud of alcohol floating in space, spanning 288 billion miles

Cats decided to live with humans on their own and domesticated themselves

Dolphins give names to each other

There are 6.8 billion people living on this planet today and only 3.5 million use a toothbrush

Over the past 500 years humans have caused 322 animal extinctions

Ronald Reagan was a lifeguard during high school during which he saved 77 lives

In colonial times lobster was considered "poverty food" and were reserved only for prisoners

Over thinking can increase anxiety and cause insomnia

The CEO of T-mobile once tweeted "AT&T and Verizon are F@#kers that are raping you"

People with brown eyes appear more trustworthy than those with blue eyes

Napoleon was once attacked by rabbits

It is actually illegal to name your child "IKEA" in Sweden

Hyenas are more closely related to cats than they are to dogs

A school in Brooklyn had to be shut down after 6th graders sprayed too much AXE Spray in a classroom, 8 students were hospitalized

Bumble bees perform small warm-up exercises before taking flight

If a Google employee passes away, their spouse gets half of their pay for 10 years

Alpacas can die of loneliness, when purchased they always need to be bought in pairs

Faking a smile has the ability to actually increase and boost your mood

Leonardo Da Vinci had such a love for animals, he would often buy caged animals just so he could set them free

Saudi Arabia banned Valentine's Day and all things red on that day

Amazon.com employees spend two days every year working at the customer service desk, including the CEO

The Ancient Romans had a festival in which the slave and slave owners would switch places

China has salamanders as large as humans

Scientists have considered whitening the clouds in order to combat global warming

Charlie Sheen once bought 2,600 seats at a baseball game just so he could catch a home run ball

If a pet owner dies in their home, a dog will wait several days to eat the corpse, a cat will only wait a day

Approximately 153,000 people will die on your birthday

Greek Yogurt is actually Turkish

One month after the nuclear bombing of Hiroshima, a typhoon hit the city killing another 2,000 people

Your nails are growing 25% faster than your grandparents' nails did

The founder of Mother's Day later fought to have it abolished

Katy Perry's father used to manufacture and sell LSD with Timothy Leary, her mother once dated Jimmy Hendrix

At age 10, Mussolini was expelled from a religious boarding school for stabbing a classmate in the hand

In the United Kingdom, accents change noticeably about every 25 miles

David Manning is a fictional critic that Sony made up to give positive reviews of their movies

Serial killer/cannibal Richard Chase only broke into houses that were unlocked – if they were locked, he thought it meant he was unwelcome

"petrichor" means the scent that lingers after a nice rain

Doctor Who introduced a dream like virtual reality in 1976, it was called "The Matrix"

The word "nightmare" is derived from "Mare" a Germanic folklore goblin who rode on peoples chests as they slept

Before he was Eminem, Marshall Mathers III was beaten so badly by a school bully he spent over a week in a coma at the age of 9

Morgan Freeman has starred in 76 films and has received 105 academy awards/nominations

In 2013 a man bought the house next door to his ex-wife so he could install a giant middle finger statue for her to see every day

Amazon ships bubble wrap in bubble wrap

A New York based nonprofit company is planning to beam free wifi to the entire world from space

Hugo Boss designed and manufactured uniforms for the Nazi Party

Continuum, a magazine that denied the existence of AIDS, went out of print in 2001 when both editors died of AIDS

Sign language has many dialects that are similar to accents; deaf people can tell where a person is from based on the way they sign

China has 64 million vacant homes, including entire cities

Most of Sony's profits come from selling insurance – In Japan they sell auto, life and medical insurance

Quentin Tarantino's IQ is the same as that of Stephen Hawking – 160

The US retail industry makes $6.8 billion a year from gift cards that no one redeems

Baboons have been known to kidnap puppies and raise them as pets

The Snickers bar was named after a horse named "Snickers"

St. Nicholas (AKA Santa Claus), is buried in Ireland

Presque Vu is the opposite of Déjà vu

Religious sites are more likely to harm your computer with viruses than porn sites

Dogs in Australia lick toads to get high

On average Google has acquired one company each week since 2010

A group of teens will be releasing an app that will allow users to report police brutality

Disney World is 20X larger than Disneyland

14 squirrels were arrested and detained in 2007 by Iranian authorities for espionage

Humans have taste buds in their stomachs, intestines, lungs and sperm

In 2006 researchers found hepatitis A in 79% of San Diego beach water samples

Scientists have created tattoos that generate electricity from sweat

75% of all cars that Rolls Royce has ever produced are still on the road today

If the earth did not have a moon our days would only be six hours long

Thousands of birds have caught fire midair above the massive solar-thermal power plant near the California-Nevada border. Employees from the plant call the dying birds "steamers" because of the trail of smoke they leave behind after igniting

You could face a $150.00 fine for failing to flush the toilet in Singapore

Robin Williams' ashes were scattered over San Francisco Bay

Ernest Hemingway, his father, his brother, his sister, and his granddaughter all committed suicide

Police were called 91 times during the filming of the movie "Borat"

Ignorant people are more likely to believe they are brilliant, while intelligent people are more likely to underestimate their abilities

Palacohol is a controversial powdered alcohol product. Just add water to the powder to make vodka or rum

If the Earth experienced a solar storm today it would disable every electrical system, leaving people in the dark for months

Canada has more lakes than the rest of the world's lakes combined

Nachos were named after the guy who created them – Ignacio Nacho Anaya

Coolio once wrote a book called "Cooking with Coolio" – Chapters included "Salad Eatin Bitches" and "Appetizers for that ass"

Jingle Bells was originally a song for Thanksgiving

Plants can get sick, they run fevers similar to humans

We are currently living in an Ice Age

Sharks are older than trees. Sharks have been around 400 million years and trees have been around only 350 million years

"Assault" is just the threat of attacking someone, " Battery" is the actual act of making unlawful contact with another

Some species of squid can fly

"Home Alone" is the highest grossing comedy film of all time

Huggies made a diaper that will tweet you when your baby soils themselves

The inventor of the speaker phone, call forwarding and conference calling died penniless and mostly unknown

Dr Seuss coined the term "nerd"

According to Hostess it takes about 45 seconds for a Twinkie to explode in a microwave

A woman in South Korea failed her driving test 771 times

Eight years worth of video is uploaded to YouTube every single day

Hiccups are the contractions of muscles that scientists say used to be gills

The final episode of "Tom and Jerry" ends with the both of them committing suicide

William Shakespeare invented "knock knock jokes"

Pistachios have been known to spontaneously combust when stored in large quantities

Most male mammals, except humans have a bone in their penis which helps them stay erect

It's possible for oysters to get herpes

In the original version of "Little Red Riding Hood" the wolf and the girl eat the flesh of her grandmother together

Terry Balsamo, guitarist for the band Evanescence, gave himself a stroke by head-banging too hard onstage

Boiling water freezes faster than cold water

There are over 200 dead bodies scattered throughout Mount Everest which now serve as landmarks on the way to the top

If the universe reaches critical velocity and begins to contract time will actually reverse

The Australian Navy will pay for boob jobs at the request of their female employees

In China you can be a professional flatulence smeller and make about $50,0000.00 USD per year

Thomas Jefferson hated banks once stating that they were "more dangerous than armies"

The year after Sudoku became popular sales of pencils increased 700%

Christopher Walken worked as a lion tamer when he was a teenager

The average player's career in the NFL is only 3.3 years

Laughter increases the activity of antibodies by about 20%, this helps destroy viruses and tumor cells

During WWII, German truck drivers thought it was good luck to drive over poop, when the British found this out, they made poop disguised bombs

The more you burp, the less you fart

California has a population larger than all of Canada

Instead of celebrating April Fool's Day the French celebrate April Fish; where they sneak up behind people and tape a paper fish to their backs

Babies are born without kneecaps

Giraffes cant cough but fish can

If a person is looking into your eyes for more than six seconds without blinking he/she either wants to kill you or have sex with you

When the candy bar 3 Musketeers was first introduced it came as three miniature bars of vanilla, strawberry and chocolate nougat centers

Kissing is healthier than shaking hands

In an emergency a Crayola crayon can be used as a candle and will burn for about 30 minutes

On January 1, 2014 it was colder in Canada than it was on Mars

The discharge of a lightning strike can leave a temporary tattoo-like marking known as a Lichtenberg

Feelings of guilt can weaken your immune system

In Finland the cost of a speeding ticket is determined by the driver's annual income

Women speak about 7,000 words a day, men average just over 2,000

McDonalds has a secret sandwich called the McGangBang, it is a McChicken sandwich in the middle of a double cheeseburger

JK Rowling is the first person to ever become a billionaire from writing books

Cows really do have best friends and become anxious when they are separated

In 1918 more than 100 waiters were arrested for poisoning bad tippers in Chicago

The average person will inhale about 44 pounds of dust in their lifetime

There are 376 Mickey Mouses hidden around the Disneyland theme park

The first man to survive going over Niagara Falls later died from slipping on an orange peel

Licking your wounds is actually beneficial – Compounds found in human saliva help speed up the healing process

In 2011 a 29 year old man became Britain's youngest grandfather when his 14 year old daughter gave birth

Before the invention of the light bulb, people slept an average of 10 hours every night

A 7'5" tall woman named Anna Bates gave birth to a 23lb baby on January 15, 1879

Lawyers in Russia threatened to sue Warner Bros. because in the Harry Potter movies, Dobby the house elf closely resembled Russian President Vladimir Putin

Japan has invented a gun that can stop people from talking

Signs that read "not responsible for your car or its contents" carry no weight in court and are posted simply to discourage legal action

Every year in the US .01% of BB gun shootings are suicide attempts

A size 8 at Banana Republic is the equivalent to a size 2 at The Gap

In the United Kingdom, young, single, childless women earn more on average than men do

A man from India started planting trees when he was 16 years old. He is now 47 and lives in his own forest with rhinos, tigers and elephants

87% of people ask questions they already know the answer to

The Nazis banned and burned the book "Bambi" because it was written by a Jewish author

Cherries can actually cause cancer cells to commit suicide

If you were to produce a sound louder than 1,100 dB, you would create a black hole and destroy the galaxy

There is an annual 100 mile foot race that is so tough only 11 people have finished the race since it began in 1985. While the date of the race is secret the entry fee is only $1.60

In the 1960s CIA field agents would occasionally prank each other by slipping the other LSD

President Jefferson hated formal affairs so much that he would often great foreign dignitaries while wearing pajamas

"Come Together" was the last song all four members of the Beatles made together

The phrase "I don't give a fuck" originated in 1790

Michigan native Barbara Soper gave birth on 08/08/08, 09/09/09 and 10/10/10.

In 2002 a garbage man won 19 million dollars, he spent it on gambling, prostitutes and drugs and today he is back being a garbage man

The world's first genetically modified babies graduated high school in 2014

A racially diverse group of people have the ability to solve problems more effectively than a group of people representing only one race in it

Ticks have been found living in the Arctic for the first time ever

The Aztec society was one of the first to require education for all its citizens regardless of gender or social status

The highest paid female CEO in the United States, Martine Rothblatt, was born a male

More music has been released by Tupac after his death than when he was alive

It takes 3000 cows to supply the NFL with enough leather for one year's supply of footballs

Marijuana has been legal in Alaska since 1975 and is still legal today

Using iTunes to build nuclear weapons is against their terms of service you agree to

Michael Jackson's autopsy revealed that his lips were tattooed pink and his eyebrows were tattooed a dark hue

If you attempt to attack or startle a vulture, it will vomit on you

It would take light 100,000 years to travel from one end of the Milky Way Galaxy to the other

Until 1987 broadcasters in the United States were legally required by the FCC to present both sides of whatever issue they were addressing

Snoop Dogg (Snoop Lion) refuses to perform at any venue unless he has a supply of 80 blunts or more

Eggs from the US are illegal in Britain because they are washed, eggs from Britain are illegal in the US because they are not washed

The CIA tried using cats as spies in the 1960s. After 5 years and 20 million dollars they weren't successful

As of 2014, three out of the last four presidents have been left handed

In 1999, hackers revealed a security flaw in Hotmail that permitted anybody to log into any Hotmail account using the password "eh"

Picasso was poor and burned most of his early work to keep his apartment warm

The average salary of a stagehand at Carnegie Hall is more than the President of the United States

The Independent Scientific Committee on drugs has found alcohol to be the most harmful drug – surpassing both heroin and crack cocaine

Chicken today contains 266% more fat and 33% less protein than it did 40 years ago

Urban Outfitters once sold "Ghettopoly" a parody of "Monopoly" that came with bonus cards that read "You got yo whole neighborhood addicted to crack, Collect $50"

Donkey and horse meat is a common ingredient in pepperoni

Millennials are on track to emerge as the most educated generation ever

Before his death Michael Jackson planned to build a 50 foot animatronics robot of himself that would wander the Las Vegas desert

In New York, Wall Street is one of the places with the highest incidences of catcalling and harassment towards women

Those who sit for most of the work day nearly double the risk of developing colon cancer

South Korea uses Xbox Kinects to detect movement on their borders

Concentration Camps were originally used by the British during the second Anglo-Boer war

Through a series of mistranslated texts, the Christian Church unwittingly accepted Buddha as a Christian saint in the middle ages

Disney rejected "Back to the Future" because they felt the mother/son storyline was not appropriate

In a 2004 song, Cookie Monster revealed that his first name is Sid

Sesame Street Ernie's song "rubber duckie" peaked at #16 on Billboard's Hot 100 singles in 1970 and was even nominated for a Grammy

"Black Friday" holds a different meaning in Australia, it refers to a series of brushfires that wiped out entire towns and killed 71 people

The government in Finland is trying to stop motorists from killing reindeer by making their antlers glow in the dark

Milk lasts twice as long when its placed in a glass container

Placing a wet paper towel around a warm beer bottle and then placing it upright in the freezer, will chill it in about two minutes

Potato chips can be used to kindle a fire

Mark Twain grew up on a farm with 20 slaves and became an abolitionist as an adult due to his affinity towards them

Graham crackers and Kellogg's Corn Flakes were originally invented to stop you from touching yourself

We can't see 20% of the universe because our own galaxy

A liter of horseshoe crab blood goes for $15,000.00 thanks to its role in sterilizing vaccines

The dragon in "Puff the Magic Dragon" was voiced by Burgess Meredith the same man who trained Rocky Balboa

Octopi have emotions and can become friends with humans

China owns all the pandas in the world any panda outside China is being leased

Hitler plotted to kill William Churchill with exploding chocolate

The world has actually gotten less violent as video games have become more violent

IKEA is working on robots that assemble their furniture for you

Britain has invaded almost 90% of the world

King Tut was mummified with an erect penis

In the first Mickey Mouse cartoons, Mickey's image is portrayed as sex-crazed and abusive to animals

While prostitution is legal in Canada, buying the services of a prostitute is not

Blue-eyed people tend to have a higher alcohol tolerance than those with darker eyes

The Hemlock water-dropwort plant is a poisonous plant that leaves the victim with a smile on their face at the time of death

Redheads require up to 20% more anesthesia to be knocked out as opposed to other people with different hair colors

Sloths only poop once a week

The "Call of Duty" video game was edited in Russia because Putin did not want Russian gamers shooting other Russians

In 2013 the last film rented out at a Blockbuster Store was the comedy "This is the End"

A "cunt hair" is the second smallest unit of measurement, used for nearly infinitesimal distances

Portugal decriminalized all drugs eleven years ago and the number of addicts has decreased 50%

Men take double the amount of selfies that women do

Scientists have discovered working Spiderman gloves that shoots webbing

Housewarming parties used to be gatherings to heat a house in the days before conventional heating

In 1939 the New York Times predicted television would fail because people would not have time to stop and stare at a screen

The day after Thanksgiving is the busiest day of the year for plumbers

The peptides in alligator blood will kill a certain strain of HIV

Coca Cola was originally green in color

Nazis invented the blow-up sex doll so that their troops wouldn't catch syphilis from prostitutes

Each of your armpits grows hair at different rates

The average bar of soap lasts twice as long as a bottle of body wash

Paris Hilton, Lady Gaga and Brad Pitt were all strippers at one point

Canada is an Indian word meaning "big village"

During WWII, Americans tried to train bats to drop bombs

In the United States, there are more cows than people

French Poodles actually originated in Germany

In the 1980s Ben and Jerry's made a rule that no employee could make more than five times what the lowest-paid worker was paid

Scientists have used stem cells to grow a tiny brain in a lab

On June 28, 2009 Stephen Hawking threw a party for time travelers. He announced the party the day after it happened and he said nobody came

In Ireland it is tradition to leave a bottle of Guinness out for Santa Claus

A man in Iowa was once arrested for attacking his pregnant wife with a McDonalds McChicken Sandwich

Of the seven wonders of the world, 3 fell due to earthquakes, 2 to fires, one probably never existed and only one still stands today

A Polish couple tried to take a selfie at the edge of a cliff and both fell to their deaths

In the late nineteenth century people thought smoking could cure asthma

In Marvel Comics, Iron Man's computer J.A.R.V.I.S. is an acronym for "just a rather very intelligent system"

Before trees were common the earth had giant mushrooms

The sons of Adolf Hitler's nephew made a pact to never have children, thus ending the Hitler bloodline

Doctor's sloppy handwriting kills more than 7000 people annually

The Pentagon has created an emergency plan in case of zombie attack

Koalas hug trees to cool off

Pink Kryptonite gives superman gay tendencies

There are pigeons trained by the US Coast Guard to spot people lost at sea

There are 328 people named "ABCDE" in the United States

Suicide is the leading cause of death among California gun purchasers

The Great Depression was so bad in the United States that Cameroon, a West African nation sent New York City $3.77 million dollars in hunger relief

Tom Hanks has an asteroid named after him "12818 Tomhanks"

Cities with a lower number of Wal-Mart stores tend to have lower crime rates

In 2001, Argentina had 5 presidents in just 10 days

Male chicks are often tossed into a grinder as babies because roosters are not as tasty as hens

The average mattress doubles in weight over the course of ten years due to the accumulation of dust mites and dust mite poop

When Neil Armstrong first walked on the moon, he carried with him pieces of the Wright Brother's first airplane

A woman in England was run off a cliff by her own flock of sheep

Neanderthals were more cognitively advanced than modern day humans

According to the Hostess Corporation, it takes about 45 seconds for a Twinkie to explode in a standard microwave

Harvard scientists recently sent the first transatlantic smell via IPhone

In the movie "A Christmas Story" Ralphie says he wants a BB gun 26 times

Sharks kill 12 people per year, humans kill 11,417 sharks per hour

There is a volcano in Indonesia that spews blue lava

In 2001 there were 70,000 adult websites in the United States, in 2011 there were 4.2 million

Cockroaches raised in space become quicker stronger faster and tougher than cockroaches raised on earth

More people commit suicide in New York City than are murdered

Grizzly bears can sniff out humans up to 18 miles away

In 1997 over 700 people in Japan experienced seizures, vomiting and eye problems after watching an episode of Pokémon

Airplane blankets are washed every five to thirty days

France banned television and radio news anchors from saying the words "Twitter" and "Face book" on air

The TSA is offering a $15,000 reward to anyone who suggests a new way to speed up airport wait times

In Italy there are about 500,000 exorcisms a year

Jingle Bells was originally a song written for Thanksgiving

During the late 13th century the word "nice" actually meant stupid and foolish

35% of British adults sleep with a teddy bear

Popular electronic store "Best Buy" was originally called "Sound of Music"

A teenager in China once sold his kidney to buy an IPad

Life emerged on Earth about 3.8 billion years ago, but sex did not evolve until more than 2 billion years later

If ants encounter a fellow ant that is intoxicated, they will carry them home to sleep it off

It takes 200 years for a human to count to 7 billion out loud

If you crack an egg underwater it will retain its original shape

Its estimated four people a year die while putting on their pants

A baby is born on it predicted due date just 4% of the time

China used more concrete in three years than the US used in the entire 20th century

In 2013, CT scans revealed that King Tut was bitten by a hippo, perhaps contributing to his death

A man named Walter Sumerford was struck by lightning 3 times during his life, even his gravestone was struck by lightning

Sunflowers can be used to clean up radioactive waste

The Philippine island of Luzon contains a lake that contains an island that contains a lake that contains another island

E.T. was voiced by a woman who smoked two packs a day, lending a unique quality to E.T.'s vocals

At weddings, the bride always stands to the left of the groom so that his sword hand is free to defend against other suitors

The modern British army has more horses than tanks

When Bono (U2) was 14, his mother died at his father's funeral

Taking magic mushrooms have been shown to help quit smoking

Face book's headquarters is located at 1 Hacker Way, Menlo Park, California

Iran is the only country in the world where it is legal to sell your kidney, the government regulates the market

Your taste buds are replaced every 10 days

Kim Jong II kidnapped a well respected movie director and forced him to make a North Korean Godzilla knock-off movie called Pulgasari

Alaska has the highest rape rate in the country

On the day Judy Garland died a huge tornado hit Kansas

If you only ate top ramen for one whole year, it would only cost you $140.00

Most of the Islamic world mourned and condemned the 9-11 attacks – Turkey left all of its flags at half mast and Iran holding candlelight vigils

There is a Greek God named Priapus – He has a permanent enormous boner

In the 19th Century it was common place to cut off some of your pubic hair and give it to a lover as a gift

Disney owns 80% of ESPN

In Spain it is believed that toasting with a glass of water will bring you seven years of bad sex

There are 1.2 Billion people on this planet who are underfed. There are 1.2 Billion people on this planet who are overweight

A Duck's quack does not echo and no one knows why

During World War II, prisoners in Canadian war camps were treated so well many of them did not want to leave when the war ended

The digestive juices inside a crocodile's stomach has the ability to dissolve steel

Leonardo Da Vinci invented scissors

A tiny amount of liquor on a scorpion will make it immediately go insane and start stinging itself

The mask used by Michael Myers in the original movie "Halloween" was a Captain Kirk mask painted white

Guinness Book of World Records holds the record for being the book most often stolen from Public Libraries

The world's second smartest man has an IQ of 192 and has spent many years as a stripper, bar bouncer, and nude model

Live lobsters are sold in vending machines in Japan

The inventor of the Lobotomy was given a Nobel Prize

In the next thirty seconds you will, on average, produce 72 million red blood cells, shed 174,000 skin cells and have 25 thoughts

The planet Neptune emits more light than it receives from the sun

According to scientists, the poop from one million Americans could contain as much as 2.6 million dollars in gold and silver

President Andrew Jackson's pet parrot was kicked out of Jackson's funeral for cursing

If you had one minute of silence for every victim of the holocaust you would be silent for eleven and a half years

New research has found that technology may be interfering with our ability to detect how others are feeling

Vin Diesel named his newborn daughter "Pauline" after the late Paul Walker

In 2014, for the first time ever, revenue from digital music downloads and subscriptions outpaced CD sales

On September 9, 2015 Queen Elizabeth II became the longest-reigning British Monarch ever, surpassing Queen Victoria

Since 2000, at least six people have been murdered after (or during) the performance of the classic Frank Sinatra song "My Way" on karaoke night

Elmer Fudd the hunter featured in many Bugs Bunny cartoons is actually a vegan and only hunts for sport

Humans put a man on the moon before they put wheels on luggage

A French company can extract the smell of your dead loved one from their clothes and make a perfume out of it

Birds that consume alcohol slur their songs, much like a human slurs their speech

Jerry of Ben and Jerry has never come up with an ice cream flavor

People in Nepal are 60 times more likely to be killed in an earthquake than people in Tokyo because Nepal's buildings aren't up to code

Panama is the only place in the world where one can see the sun rise on the Pacific Ocean and set in the Atlantic Ocean

One of the earliest, precisely dated recorded events is two guys getting drunk on October 22, 2137BC

George Washington is the only US President to have received 100% of the electoral votes

Russian ruler Peter III once hanged a large rat in public because it had eaten his toy soldiers, he was 25 at the time

Coca-Cola and Pepsi are used as pesticides by farmers in India because they are cheaper and get the job done

During an experiment at New York University, a robotic fish was accepted by other fish and became their leader

In Victorian days "crinkum-crankum" was a slang word for vagina and "tallywag" was slang for penis

If Iron Man suit is really made out of a gold titanium alloy then his suit would weigh 350 lbs

USA has 19 aircraft carriers, the rest of the world has 12 combined

Al Capone hated the nickname "Scarface" and preferred the names "Big Fellow" and "Snorky" given to him by other criminals

Karl Marx named all four of his daughters "Jenny"

In ancient Egypt pyramid builders inscribed their crew's nicknames on the bricks (for example "The friends of Khufu Gang" and "The Drunkards of Menkuare")

You can run for president while in prison

A woman in a wheelchair, who had no feet, won a treadmill on the "Price is Right "

Nikola Tesla developed the idea for Smartphone technology in 1901

At one point the Statue of Liberty became a giant battery due to its paint and metal being exposed to salt water

Poor people are more generous than rich people

In the first three months of 2015, pirates kidnapped over 140 hostages

Taco Bell started off as a hot dog stand

People who pirate movies and music actually spend more money on media than people who purchase everything legally – about 30% more

A man in Saudi Arabia has installed a fridge in the street and stocked it with free food for homeless people

When the moon is directly above you, you weigh less

During the 20th Century horses were creating so much pollution with their poop that automobiles were seen as the "green" alternative

---

President Andrew Jackson was involved in as many as 100 duels, most of which were fought to defend his wife's honor

The day after Robin William's suicide, the National Suicide Prevention Lifeline fielded the highest number of calls in its history

George Foreman named all five of his sons George Foreman

In 2009 Australian wildlife authorities deployed snipers to protect a colony of penguins from predators

In 2011 China aired clips of the movie "Top Gun" on their local news and tried to pass it off as if the Chinese Air Force was doing training exercises

In 2012, a six year old girl threw a temper tantrum so extreme she was handcuffed and taken to jail from her kindergarten class

The cereal "Cookie Crisp" is created by Purina, a pet food company

A man named Thomas Earl was once fired from his job, mauled by a bear, and shot by the police all in the same day

Theophilus Van Kannel invented revolving doors because he hated opening doors for women

Science claims that on average a cyclist can go 70 seconds faster if they have shaved legs

 Tricking someone into viewing obscene material online is a crime that could land the perpetrator ten years in prison

Led Zepplin, Depeche Mode and REM never had a number one single

Before they moved to LA the Dodgers hailed from Brooklyn and got their name from Brooklyn's extremely deadly and fast moving street cars – The "Brooklyn Trolley Dodgers"

"Pocahontas" Native American nickname means "the naughty child" or "spoiled one"

The town of Tikrit in Iraq has erected a monument of the shoe that was thrown at president George W. Bush

In 2010, due to a border error on Google maps, Nicaragua accidentally invaded Costa Rica

A Korean man was once killed by a live octopus he swallowed, the octopus latched onto his throat with its tentacles and suffocated him

A brownout refers to when you get drunk and don't remember portions of your night until someone else refreshes you

Honey bees are assigned jobs by other honey bees based on their age

If you have a fear of something and then label it or give it a name, it becomes easier to control

As a young teenager, Osama Bin Laden formed an acapella singing group with some of his friends

Cap' n Crunch's full name is Horatio Magellan Crunch and the number of stripes on uniform indicate the rank of Commander and not Captain

Because of the Chernobyl disaster, radioactive hogs now roam around Germany

You can be fined up to $1000.00 for using Silly String on Halloween in Hollywood

Not a single cactus grows in the Sahara Desert, since cacti are only native to the Americas

During the late 19th Century, it was popular for wealthy families to host mummy-unwrapping parties using real Egyptian mummies

There are only 22 countries in the world that the British have not invaded or attacked

McDonalds opened the first Ski-thru fast food restaurant in Lindvallen, Sweden

Over 98% of insecticides and 95% of herbicides do not reach their target destination

DNA has a 521 year half-life, meaning genetic material can't be recovered from dinosaurs and "Jurassic Park" is impossible

Godzilla is an official citizen of Japan

In 2013 a feral pig in Australia stole 18 beers from a campsite, got drunk, and then tried to fight a cow

Will Smith is now older than Uncle Phil was at the beginning of "The Fresh Prince of Bel-Air"

In 2015, an agoraphobic woman who had ventured out of her house only twice in ten years briefly stepped out of her home and fell into an open manhole

Since WWII, 400 descendants of Nazis have converted to Judaism and moved to Israel

The state of Alabama spent $750000 in taxpayer money to obtain the rights to the song "Sweet Home Alabama"

You can ripen a sour mango by soaking it in warm water for 10 minutes

Scientists have developed a real-life tractor beam that can force objects closer or further to it

The United Kingdom uses "incident screens" that block the view of a traffic accident from other drivers on the road in an attempt to reduce delays

In the 16th Century people believed that water opened the pores in their skin which allowed dangerous diseases into the body, therefore most never took baths

Bruce Lee was able to perform one hand push-ups using only his index finger and thumb

20% of the Population in Poland died during WWII, the highest percent of any nation

Nelson Mandela co-authored a book with Fidel Castro

The inventor of the contact lens Adolf Fick, got his idea when popcorn kernels kept getting stuck in his teeth

63 earths could fit inside Uranus

After three years the Police in the state of Ohio have finally caught a serial pooper, who has pooped on at least 22 cars

Americans consume over 100 million M&Ms every day

A Pine tree planted in 2004 in memory of former Beatle George Harrison died after it was infested by beetles

The CDC estimates that in the United States cows kill 22 people every year… and 75% of those are known to have been deliberate attacks

Moldy bread is useful disinfecting cuts and dates back as far back as ancient Egypt

North Korea is the only country that has been caught cheating at the International Mathematical Olympiad… Twice

The United Kingdom includes Northern Ireland, Great Britain does not

China is one of the suicide capitals of the world, they employ body fishers – People who are hired to drag dead bodies out of rivers

Before coffee became popular beer was often served for breakfast in the United States

Stephen Hawking thinks aliens exist

During WWII a Dutch warship disguised itself as a tropical island to escape detection by the Japanese and became the only ship of its class to survive

Ancient Rome briefly had a population of one million around 200 AD, no other western city would reach that number until 1,600 years later

In 1994, a 75 pound bag of cocaine fell out of a plane and landed in the middle of a Florida crime watch meeting

Miami is the only major United States city that was founded by a woman

Eggo Waffles were originally called "Froffles" a combination of the word "frozen" and "waffles"

The highest mountain in Texas has a stainless steel pyramid at its summit

Wet hay bales can spontaneously combust when stored improperly

George Washington preferred not to shake the hands of visitors, he would bow instead

Lewis Hawkins, a 54 year old gang member once had his mother drive him to an apartment so he could shoot someone

The city of Colma, CA has 1,000 times more dead residents than living: 1,400 living and 1.5 million dead

Wallace Souza, a Brazilian TV Personality who hosted a true-crime TV show, arranged murders himself trying to get the inside scoop and boost ratings

The Dallas Cowboys stadium uses more electricity than the entire country of Liberia

There have been two known fatalities of people suffocating on marshmallows while playing the game "Chubby Bunny"

The Ouija Board got its name by a medium asking the board what it should be called

It is predicted that in our Milky Way Galaxy alone there are over 500 million planets capable of supporting life

By law no United States officer is allowed to outrank George Washington, who posthumously became a six-star general

In the four decades between 1970 and 2012 marine species have declined 49 percent

The Aztec Empire used chocolate as currency – One hen was worth 100 cacao beans

The IKEA headquarters in the Netherlands has to stop serving its cheap breakfast because the highways could not handle the traffic

Plants can get cancer

An Amazonian ant called *Mycocepurus smithii* reproduces through cloning. No male of the species have ever been found

Freshwater fish do not drink water, it enters through the gills but saltwater fish must drink tons of water and filter out the salt

Denmark has more pigs than people

In 2015 a debate team from New York's Eastern Correctional Facility (a prison) beat the national debate championship team from Harvard University

A London based designer created a lamp shaped like a butt, it turns on when someone slaps or pinches it

A study shows that Ravens are able to work together to achieve a common goal, but will not cooperate if they know their partner to be a cheater

New York City makes 33 million tons of trash per year, more than double the waste created by Tokyo Japan, which holds 12 million more people

The city of Idyllwild has had actual Golden Retrievers that serve as Mayors of the city since 2012

The largest city in the world inaccessible by roads is Inquitos, Peru. It has a population of 400,000 people and is located deep in the Amazon rainforest

The last words Abraham Lincoln heard was "You sockdologizing old man-trap" a punch-line from the play 'Our American Cousin'

The average American picks his/her nose four times per day

Up to half of all incoming mobile calls made to New York City's 911 call centers are the result of accidental butt dialing

The 2015 graduating class of the NYPD Police Academy had the lowest percentage of black graduates not seen since the 1960s

A number of churches in Europe have claimed to possess the "Holy Prepuce" or Jesus' foreskin. It is said to have miraculous powers

A Post Office located in Bedrock, Colorado gets so much Flintstone fan mail that they have a "return to sender – Fictitious Cartoon Character" stamp

Nobody knows who first named our planet "Earth"

Prince Charles owns an Aston Martin that runs on wine

In Nashville, TN there is a five-story fully automated vending machine that dispenses real cars

There is an island that Canada and Denmark have been fighting over for years. Each country sends their militaries to remove each other's flag

As of 2010 residents of the UK are the only ones allowed to go inside Big Ben Tower and you have to be sponsored by a member of parliament

Pound for pound the spice Saffron is more expensive then gold

The state of Florida is 15,409 square miles larger than England

In Brooklyn, NY you can rent a Mom for $40.00, she gives advice, listens, cooks and helps with chores

In Bhutan it is believed that evil spirits can't bend their bodies, therefore homes in Bhutan are built with small doorways forcing guests to bend over while walking in

South Florida is the only place in the world where alligators and crocodiles co-exist

Due to China's newly lax lawsuit rules a man in Shanghai is suing popular Chinese actress Zhao Wei for staring at him too hard through the television

17th and 18th Century German families hung their Christmas trees upside down, which was said to engulf the tree with divine powers

You have the right to put on your resume that in 2006 you were awarded TIME Magazines "Person of the Year". In 2006, TIME Magazine chose 'Everyone' as their "Person of the Year"

Asian-American women and Hispanic men are more likely than any other racial or ethnic group to sustain long-term marriages

All humans collectively poop approximately 2,299,421,390 pounds of excrement every day

In the UK, if you hit a dog with your car you must immediately report it to the Police, but not a cat

"The Very Hungry Caterpillar" has sold a copy somewhere in the world every single minute since the day it was first published

Cuba Gooding Jr's father was banned from the set of Jerry Maguire for asking Tom Cruise if he was gay or not

Drinking too many IPAs can cause "man boobs" the more hops create more estrogen in humans

Beluga Whales blow an average 58 bubbles per minute, the shape of the bubbles they create depends on their mood

During WWI, the British army trained seagulls to poop on periscopes of enemy submarines

---

In 1980 Saddam Hussein was given the key to the city of Detroit

There are roughly 10 million more baby boys than girls born worldwide every year

British people say "Happy Christmas" because in the 19th Century the word 'happy' became more high-class than the word 'merry'

There is a town in Norway called Hell; it freezes over almost every winter

The first person executed in the Massachusetts Bay Colony was guilty of sex with a mare, a cow, two goats, two calves and a turkey

Alice Cooper used to babysit Keanu Reeves

4% of the sand on Normandy beaches is made up of shrapnel from D-Day landings, broken down over the decades into sand-sized chunks

It requires 7 to 8 trees to provide enough oxygen for just one person per year

Saudi Arabia imports their camels from Australia

In the 1700s, a pirate ship hoisting a black flag meant that if a vessel surrendered its goods, the pirates were willing to spare its crew

The closest habitable planet is said to be just 14 light years away and is twice the size of Earth

The Ancient Romans substituted criminals into plays for punishment, so if a character died in the plays story, a real criminal would die onstage

Before the Post Office started accepting letters from Santa, kids yelled their Christmas wishes up the chimney or tied their notes to balloons

Brenda Lee was 13 years old when she recorded "Rockin' Around the Christmas Tree"

The Magnetic North Pole, once located over Canada, is now in the Arctic Ocean and is slowly moving towards Russia

A hug that lasts for 20 seconds releases oxytocin, which can strengthen trust between two people

Mathew McConaughey's brother, Rooster McConaughey, named his son Miller Lite and got free beer for a year

There are currently 48 real princesses in the world

Eating too many Flaming Hot Cheetos can send you to the emergency room with gastritis, an inflamed stomach lining

On average, zero tampons a year are sold to women in Turkey, Nigeria, Kenya, Morocco, Thailand and United Arab Emirates

It takes 95% less energy to recycle aluminum than it does to make it from raw materials

There are people actually living in the Mos Eisley Cantina set from Star Wars

Vatican City is the only country in the world in which women cannot vote

In rich countries, obesity is more common among the less educated but in poor countries, obesity is more common among the highly educated

A lab in London has created an edible water bottle that leaves virtually no waste behind

As a symbol of unity between their two countries, King Phillip II of France and King Richard I of England slept in the same bed

Each In-and-Out Burger Stand must be within 600 miles of where the burger patties are made, nothing is ever frozen or micro-waved

From 2011 to 2014 the US Department of Defense paid 14 NFL teams $5.4 million to salute the troops during their broadcasts

Austin Texas is the most populous city in the United States without a pro sports team

Benihana, which is Japanese for "red safflower" was named after a flower that survived a WWII bombing in Japan

Nicolas Cage once voluntarily returned a Tyrannosaur Rex skull he bought for $276,000.00 to the Mongolian Government after learning it had been stolen

Montana is the only state in the US whose constitution mandates teaching Native American tribal history

In September of 2015, a Costco shopper punched another shopper in the face over samples of Nutella waffles

Some of the 'Miller Coors' beers still use yeast descended from the supply the founder brought over with him from Europe in 1855

Before becoming a comic book creator, Stan Lee wrote obituaries for celebrities in New York

Egyptian billionaire Naguib Sawirs is attempting to buy an island from Greece or Italy to house refugees

The State of Oklahoma's Capitol Building is the only one that sits on an active oil well. There is even an oil rig out in front of the building

Ninjas used egg shells as weapons – They would drain the egg and replaced it with irritants such as ashes, salt or powdered pepper

Research shows that there is no such thing as a "male" or "female" brain. All human brains contain male-like and female-like features

When Sky diver Joan Murray's parachute failed to open she hit the ground traveling around 81 miles an hour, then, she landed on a mound of fire ants and was stung over 200 times. The shock from being stung repeatedly by the ants released a surge of adrenaline which in turn kept her heart beating and she survived

Sir Isaac Newton died a virgin

A group of Pandas is called an "embarrassment"

Napoleon was buried without his penis

Tylenol can numb not only physical pain but emotional pain as well

A 32,000 year old extinct Arctic flower was resurrected using seeds found by an Ice Age squirrel

In 1904 Carl Emil Pettersson (a Swedish sailor) found himself shipwrecked on an island in Papua New Guinea. The island was inhabited by a cannibalistic tribe who captured the sailor and brought him to the King. The King's daughter immediately fell in love with Carl and he married the Kings daughter. After the Kings death Carl became King of the island.

Today's nuclear waste retains 95% of its energy, which means the nuclear waste that exists today could power the entire planet for 72 years

Flint, Michigan accidentally gave its entire population lead poisoning when the water supply was switched to the Flint River to save money

The people of Hawaii consume about 7 million cans of SPAM per year, 5 million pounds in total

For the first time in 20 years Seattle cleaned its' famous Gum Wall, which had an estimated one million chewed wads of gum stuck to it

Dubai has equipped their first responders and rescue workers with jetpacks, since the city holds some of the world's tallest skyscrapers

Quantum teleportation has been achieved

In January 2016, two Russian men died while taking a selfie. They were holding a hand grenade with the pin pulled out. The cell phone and pictures survived the explosion

New Horizons is the fastest spacecraft ever launched traveling 10 miles per second

George Lucas originally wanted Han Solo to be a large green gilled fish monster

Reed College in Portland Oregon is the only liberal arts college in the world that has a nuclear reactor run by undergraduate students

The United States is the first country to explore every planet in the solar system

Free Willy died one year after being released into the wild

John Hancock attended the coronation of King George II and met the monarch. 15 years later King George II put a 500 pound bounty on John Hancock's head

NASA's Curiosity Rover team has taken photos of the first 'petrified' sand dunes on Mars

The average healthy human lifespan is equal to one year on Uranus

Some snakes can survive without food up to two years at a time by digesting their own hearts

In 1900, 40% of American automobiles were powered by steam, 38% by electricity

There are two geysers at the heart of the Milky Way Galaxy that contain enough energy equivalent to a million exploding stars

The Newfoundland dog is from Labrador and the Labrador dog is from Newfoundland

Studies find that happiness is 10% life circumstances, 50% genetics and 40% attitude

The train used as Hogwarts Express in the Harry Potter movies is an actual train that runs through Scotland

In 1915 professional Doctors believed that a menstruating woman could kill an entire colony of bees with her stare

In order to fund their sea voyage to get to the 1932 Olympics, Brazilian athletes loaded their ship up with coffee and sold it as they made their way to Los Angeles, California

Benito Mussolini's granddaughter is currently a member of the Italian parliament

North Korea is currently bombarding South Korea with balloons filled with used toilet paper, tissues and cigarette butts

There is a giant lavender labyrinth in Michigan that can be seen from Google Earth
In 1984 the creator of the font Papyrus signed away his rights for $835.00, as of 2012 Papyrus font was on the machines of at least one billion people

In the United States, tortillas outsell hamburger buns, hotdog buns, and all other fresh types of rolls, buns, croissants and bagets

Before Groundhog Day became a popular holiday in the United States, the French used a marmot, the English used a hedgehog and the Germans used a badger

Albert Einstein died after refusing life-saving surgery. He said "I want to go when I want, it is tasteless to prolong life artificially, I have done my share, it is time to go, I will do it elegantly

A study found that Tropical countries are twice as likely to have a civil war in years that have been preceded by and El Nino weather system

The FDA approved the first genetically modified animal destined for human consumption, a fast-growing salmon

There are scholarships just for redheads

Steve Jobs claimed that taking LSD was one of the most important things he had ever taken in his lifetime

Kobe Bryant holds the record for the most missed shots in the NBA

Our brains take only three hundredths of a second to decide a person's trustworthiness

LEGO sets have been a better investment than gold since the year 2000

More than 50,000 people in Japan today are over 100 years old

Floridian Joshua James was recently arrested after throwing a 3.5 foot alligator through the drive-thru window of a Wendy's restaurant

R. Norris Williams survived the sinking of the Titanic but spent so much time submerged in the icy waters that doctors wanted to amputate his legs. He refused and later, that same year, went on to win the US Tennis championship

An NFL water boy makes an average salary of $53,000.00 per year

The biggest regret that people have on their deathbeds is that they lived the life expected of them instead of the life true to themselves

Before becoming Prime Minister of the United Kingdom, Tony Blair spent a brief period pursuing a career as a stand-up comic

The official inventor of the Fire Hydrant is unknown because the original patent was burned in a fire

Drug lord Pablo Escobar got to build his own prison; it featured a soccer field, a giant doll house, a bar, a Jacuzzi and a waterfall

More than 3000 Bible prophecies have YET to come true, but 3,200 have already been fulfilled

Napoleon Bonaparte and Adolf Hitler were born 129 years apart, they rose to power 129 years apart and they both declared war on Russia 129 years apart

During his tenure as a congressman and later as President of the United States, John F. Kennedy donated all of his salary to charities

The fifth oldest tree on the planet was burned to the ground when a woman was caught smoking meth

Sigmund Freud recommended cocaine as treatment for alcoholism, morphine addiction, and depression

Natalie Portman has been published in two scientific journals

Anywhere between 5-15% of the bombs dropped over Europe during WWII never exploded and are still hidden where they fell

US President Gerald Ford would blame his farts on his Secret Service people saying things like "Jesus, was that you? Show some class!"

Alcohol helps to fight off radioactive poisoning – Most of the survivors of Chernobyl were drunk at the time of the Nuclear Disaster

There is a fake slum-like African resort designed to give rich people a taste of the hard life. It is a shanty town equipped with under-floor heating and Wi-Fi

Beards can slow the aging process by stopping water from leaving the skin, keeping it moisturized

On October 28, 2013 wind power not only provided 100% of Denmark's power but at 2:00 AM Denmark wind was producing 122% of the country's energy needs

Pluto was discovered to have floating hills. The dwarf planet's famous "heart" is made up of clusters of water-ice hills that float in a sea of frozen nitrogen

Dr. Ruth a sex therapist is also a trained sniper. Her family was killed during the Holocaust and at the age of 16 she moved to Israel and joined the Jewish military.

According to research the older the father is when he has a child, the uglier the child will be

Briefly George Washington stopped the Revolutionary War to return a lost dog to the enemy. A British Generals' terrier was found wandering the battlefield when Washington ordered a cease fire. The US waved a truce flag and both sides stopped shooting until the dog was returned to the British commander

In 2010 famous stoner Cheech Marin beat Anderson Cooper (a Yale Graduate) and Aisha Tyler (Dartmouth Graduate) in Celebrity Jeopardy. He won with a score of $10,200 while the other two tied with $0

In 1993 a man from Missouri named James Scott purposely damaged a levee on the Mississippi River to delay his wife coming home from work so he could party. Instead, the river flooded 14,000 acres, the man was later arrested convicted of causing a catastrophe and sentenced to life in prison

There is a statue of Nikola Tesla in Silicon Valley that broadcasts a free WIFI signal

The German Parliament building has a glass dome above it that people are allowed to walk over. This is to remind politicians that the government should be transparent and the people are always above them

A Colombian woman once found a potato growing in her vagina

The best time to buy a plane ticket is 54 days before takeoff in order to get the lowest prices

Several days after the death of TV and Radio personality Jack Benny, his widow received a red rose. Another rose was delivered to her every day after that. Mary called to find out who was sending them and the florist told her that Jack had made arrangements for a rose to be delivered to her every day for the rest of her life

Government vehicles in Cuba are legally required to pick up hitchhikers if there is available space

Under the right conditions it is physically possible for a planet to be shaped like a doughnut

In 1913 Adolf Hitler, Joseph Stalin, Leon Trotsky and Sigmund Freud all lived within a few miles of each other in Vienna, with some of them being regulars at the same coffee shop

After four millennia of erosion the Great Pyramid of Giza has shrunk about 25 feet

At least seven taxi drivers in Northwest Japan have reported picking up the ghost of a person who died in the 2011 Earthquake/Tsunami

Mid-century American Lawyers have spent over 12 years arguing about what percentage of peanuts constitutes real peanut butter

Thirteen US Presidents have come and gone while Queen Elizabeth II has been on the throne

"Finding Nemo" is the best selling DVD of all time

Alex the African grey parrot was the first and only non-human animal to ask an existential question. He asked what color he was and learned that he was grey

Psychopaths can only think of the possible positive consequences of their actions, not the negative ones

The Bible never uses the word 'apple' when referring to the forbidden fruit. Some believe it was a grape, fig, pomegranate or mushroom

The French Government is planning on building 620 miles of solar pavement, which will provide power for up to 8% of the country's population

THC has 20 times the anti-inflammatory power of aspirin

The first time Japanese citizens ever heard their Emperors voice was on the radio where he announced the surrender of his country in WWII

Chinchilla fur is so dense that fleas and other skin parasites will suffocate if they try to live in it

In 202 BC the Han Dynasty of China was already drilling for natural gas, transporting it in pipelines and burning it in stoves

When a massive power outage struck southern California in the late 1990s Los Angeles residents called 911 to express concern about the strange clouds hovering above them, those residents were explained to that they were seeing the Milky Way for the first time

Water, gas and electricity has been free in Turkmenistan since 1991

The town of Dildo Newfoundland has an annual festival called Dildo Days, which is led by their mascot Captain Dildo

Before Bill Nye became the Science guy he won a Steve Martin lookalike contest

81 year old Luciano Mares caught a mouse in his home and threw the mouse into a pile of burning leaves in order to kill it. While on fire, the mouse ran back into the house setting his entire house on fire destroying everything

When zooplankton eat plastics their poop takes longer to fall to the bottom of the ocean, resulting in more marine life eating toxic plastic

All the loose change Americans left at airport security in 2014 equals $674,841.06 and the TSA got to keep it all

Jim Carrey was supposed to play the role of Dr. Evil in the franchise Austin Powers but had to back out due to scheduling conflicts

In 70% of the world, girls outperform boys in educational achievement

Technically both pronunciations of the word 'Celtic" is correct

The 2015 Census in Japan shows that the population has shrunk by nearly one million people in the past five years, the first decline since 1920

Today there are two operational robots on the surface of Mars and five operational orbiters circling the planet

There is an A.I. that makes telemarketers believe they are talking to a real person, wasting much of their time and money as possible

The Manchineel is one of the most dangerous trees. The sap from its trunk can give you blisters, eating its apples can kill you, and if you try and burn it the smoke can make you blind

The film Deadpool was released in February 2016, exactly twenty-five years after Deadpools first appearance in New Mutants #98 comic

North Korea's newest satellite passed over Super Bowl 50 an hour after it had ended

At LEGO fan conventions "One by Five" is code for a hot girl, because hot girls at a LEGO convention are rare and LEGO does not make a 1X5 piece

A newborn baby was abandoned in a forest in Kenya for two days and was eventually found by a stray dog looking for food. The dog carried the infant across a busy road, through a barbed wire fence to its litter of puppies. The baby was found in that litter brought to a hospital without a bruise.

A new rock opera about Ancient Roman Emperor Nero will be staged directly atop the underground ruins of the emperor's actual residence

A charging elephant burst through the front door of a home in India but stopped immediately when it heard a baby cry inside. The elephant removed the debris that it had caused using its trunk and returned to the forest

75% of all current female senators were in the Girl Scouts growing up and so was every female secretary of state

The oldest hotel in the world has been operated by the same Japanese family for over 1,300 years and has been cared for by 52 generations of descendants

There is a secret swimming pool somewhere in the Mojave Desert that anyone who finds it can use

A man named Robert Lane named his two sons Winner and Loser. Winner grew up to be a criminal and Loser became a Police Detective

New York City's Washington Square Park was used as a graveyard from 1797-1825, it is believed up to 20,000 bodies lie beneath the park and bodies are routinely found during excavations

Avocados are toxic to almost every other animal except humans

Europe has banned more than half of all cosmetics that Americans use on a daily basis due to health risks

Uber is now worth more money than General Motors

The lone Japanese passenger who survived the Titanic sinking was marked a coward by his country for not dying with the other Japanese passengers

The Powerpuff Girls were originally called Whoopass Girls

The difference between terror and horror is that terror occurs in anticipation of the horrifying experience, while horror occurs afterwards

An entire village was built on the coast of Malta for the movie Popeye in 1980, it still stands today

The skull that the Russians kept as evidence of Hitler's death is actually the skull of a woman

Rent for a hot dog cart near New York's Central Park Zoo is $289,500.00 a year which is more than an apartment rental in the same neighborhood

Your fingerprint is not protected under the 5th Amendment so police can force you to unlock a phone with a fingerprint but not a password

From 1887 up until 1950, U.S. weather forecasters were forbidden from attempting to predict tornadoes

The driest place on earth is the Atacama Desert in Chile. In 2015 the area received record amount of rainfall and weeks later the entire desert blossomed in pink flowers

It is illegal to abandon your parents in China. Anyone whose parents over 60 is legally required to visit them often and make sure their needs, financially and spiritually are being met

There are 84 people in the United States named LOL

The sons of Hitler's nephew who fought for the United States both made a pact never to have children so they could end Hitler's bloodline

Bearded Vultures wear makeup. They show their social status by rubbing their bodies in iron rich soil staining their white feathers red

There are one billion cattle in the world, 200,000,000 of those cattle are in India where the slaughter of cows is largely illegal

Nikola Tesla developed the idea for smart phone technology in 1901

In 1987 Kenneth Parks killed his mother-in-law, assaulted his father-in-law and drove to the Police Station to confess and he did this all in his sleep

1835 the US became debt free, that was the last time

Teenager Michelle Carter was charged with manslaughter after she sent texts encouraging her boyfriend to commit suicide, and he did.

In 1994 Los Angeles Police arrested a man for dressing up as the Grim Reaper and standing outside the windows of old peoples' homes

Mark Zuckerberg purchased all four homes surrounding his house in order to ensure his privacy, for a total of 30 million

Koi fish can live for centuries one is recorded to have lived to be 226 years old

James Capone, Al Capone's brother worked as a federal prohibition agent

A soldier of the Indian Army once fought off 40 train robbers with a knife, killing 3 and injuring 8 to save a girl from getting raped

Kiko the dog sensed a diabetes-related infection in her owner's big toe and chewed it off while he was drunk, saving his life

Bob Marley never won a Grammy while he was alive but collectively his children have won 13

A man named Joseph Bolitho Johns escaped Australian prison so many times, they built a special cell just for him and he later escaped that.

Brown colored eyes are really blue, under a layer of melanin

Your body is creating and killing 15 million red blood cells per second

Actress Hedy Lamarr was once considered the most beautiful woman in the world. She was also a mathematician and inventor of the frequency hopping spread spectrum technology that's used in Bluetooth and WIFI. Her idea was brushed off and others took credit for it. She spent her entire life wishing people would acknowledge her brains instead of just her beauty

The term once in a blue moon literally means 2-3 years

During the filming of the Harry Potter movies Daniel Radcliffe was nicknamed "Harry Puffer" by his co-stars for having a so-called 20-a-day cigarette habit

In 2008, a 30 second Doritos television advertisement was beamed by radar to a solar system 42 light years away

King Kong was the very first movie to have a sequel

Charles Rigoulot a French weightlifter was put in jail for hitting a Nazi guard. He ended up breaking out of jail by bending the bars and helped others escape as well, then beat up the guard who jailed him

People born between 1997-1999 have lived in three decades, two centuries, and two millenniums

Smell is by far the strongest sense that can evoke past memories and emotions

The Lion King will forever hold the record as the best selling VHS tape of all time, with over 50 million copies sold

A train ran over and killed a couple in South Africa while they were having sex on the tracks

The word "dude" was first used in the 1800s as an insult towards young men who were too concerned with keeping up with the latest fashions

Some caterpillars can launch their own poop up to two meters in order to defend themselves from predators

Scientists once put mice in a maze and exposed them to loud heavy metal music. The mice did not finish the maze, instead they killed each other

97% of people do not know that Osama Bin Laden was a CIA agent during the 1980s

In 2010 the Foo Fighters Dave Grohl was hospitalized after he overdosed… on coffee

Disney is currently using "anti-drone" drones to prevent people from spying on the set of Star Wars Episode VIII

In 2010 McDonalds mistakenly packed and distributed 5,000 Happy Meals with a condom instead of a toy

The Steve Miller Band and Journey were both comprised of former members of the 60s psychedelic rock band Frumious Bundersnatch

The average citizen in Liechtenstein doesn't even lock their door because crime in their country is so low their last murder was in 1997

Young Isaac Newton once threatened to burn his mother and stepfather alive

There are spiders in Australia big enough to eat snakes

There's a pill that makes farts smell like chocolate

London has the most billionaires of any city in the world

Gerry Hoy was trying to prove that the glass in the Toronto-Dominion Centre was unbreakable; he threw himself against the glass wall and fell 24 stories to his death when the frame gave way

Recently researchers have discovered a 100-foot long tunnel that confirms one of the greatest escapes from the Holocaust. The tunnel was dug with only spoons and bare hands and was completed in three months.

There is a secret apartment at the top of the Eiffel Tower

President Hoover asked every American to turn off their lights for one minute in October 1931, as a tribute to the death of Thomas Edison

Martha Stewart became a billionaire while she was in prison

There is a mountain in Australia called Mt. Disappointment, named after explorers found the view from the mountain to be sub-par and wanted to reflect that

In 1977 a 13 year old boy found a tooth growing out of his foot

A solar flare nearly destroyed planet Earth on July 23, 2012 but no one knew about it

In Austria, you can go swimming in pools of beer

Musician Ed Sheeran"s childhood friend Amy Wedge could not pay her mortgage so Ed let her co-write "thinking out loud" to earn money

Justin Timberlake's "Rock your Body" was intended for Michael Jackson's final album, Invincible

It would take 200 years for a human being to count to 7 billion out loud

Ants can survive inside a working microwave because the ants are small enough to dodge the rays

If you are at a restaurant wash your hands after ordering, the menu is generally the dirtiest thing you can touch

HP Printer Black Ink is more expensive than human blood

There are enough diamonds in existence to give everyone on the planet a cupful

Pigeons can't fart

The tree where Sir Isaac Newton discovered gravity is still standing, alive and well, outside of his childhood home

Ivan Mishukov left his abusive parents house at the age of four and lived with a pack of wild dogs. Before being captured by police, he became the pack's leader and escaped authorities three times. He ended up going to military school and today is serving in the Russian Army

Chocolate milk was invented in Jamaica

A pet penguin named LaLa walks into town by himself with a backpack every day to collect fish from the local market

Charlie from the original Willy Wonka movie never acted in another movie after that. He became a large animal veterinarian

The person who invented the stop sign, pedestrian crossing sign, the traffic circle, and the one-way street never learned how to drive

Metallica is the first and only band to play on all seven continents

The Doctor who discovered that hand washing prevented the spread of disease was thrown into a mental institution for his crazy ideas

A rotund Santa Claus with a white beard and red clothing that we are used to today was actually created by Coca Cola

High School students in 2016 have the same anxiety levels as insane asylum patients in the 1950s

Marijuana is the oldest natural, purest, and healthiest pain relief medication in the world. Its use dates back to 10 B.C.

The average amount of time a woman can keep a secret is 47 hours and 15 minutes

The ability to digest alcohol occurred 10 million years ago and many researchers believe it played a key role in our own evolution

"Seinfeld" has made $2.7 Billion since it went off the air in 1998

Mark Linaker of Ginger's Grill in Prestatyn, Wales is giving a 20% discount to customers with red hair because "They deserve a break"

The sum of all numbers on a roulette wheel is 666

A 7th grader was given an assignment to trace her lineage, decided to put together a massive Presidential Family Tree and found that every single US President except Martin Van Buren is related to the King of England

The Masaya Volcano, located in Managua, Nicaragua is getting WI-FI. Researchers are installing it to better predict the volcano's eruptions

People in China refer to Katy Perry as "Fruit Sister"

Johnny Knoxville in 2007, injured his penis so bad that he has to use a catheter twice a day

Coca Cola says that there are only two people on the planet that know the recipe for Coca Cola. Those two are not allowed to fly on the same plane in case it crashes

Sunburn is the result of your skin cells committing mass suicide to protect you from their damaged DNA, which can cause cancer

More billionaires were born in New York City than anywhere else in the world

A video game developer once snuck a proposal to his girlfriend into a video game, but his girlfriend refused to play the game for years, delaying their eventual marriage

Mice were exposed to heavy metal music during a study to see how it affects them. Instead of completing the maze the mice killed each other

Arnold Schwarzenegger has punched the most animals in movies. Will Ferrell is a close second.

"Holy Smoke" is a company that turns a person's cremated remains into shotgun shells

Huggies has made a diaper that will tweet you when your child soils themselves

In the original story of "The Little Mermaid" Ariel does not marry the prince. The prince marries someone else and Ariel kills herself

Atheism is punishable by death in at least 13 countries

Tom Cruise voiced Captain Planet in a few episodes but was kicked off the show for wanting more control of what topics where explored

A major league pitcher confessed to pitching every game over a 12 year career high on drugs, including a no-hitter while high on LSD

"Light Rose Garden" is a public art installation of over 25,000 LED roses that were on display in Chengdu, China until October 2016

No Egyptian president has left office without being arrested or dead

A guy from a Canadian Island has sent over 4000 messages in a bottle and has received over 3000 responses from people all over the world

A man threatening to jump from a South Carolina bridge was convinced to stop with a pizza

Vogue magazine has banned models that are too skinny, underage or appear to have an eating disorder

The carbon dioxide released by humans is slowly turning the ocean into acid

The Outer Space Treaty of 1967 made it illegal for countries to establish military bases on the moon

In 2015, two day care employees in New Jersey were imprisoned for running a toddler "fight club" among dozens of boys and girls aged 4-6

Mary, the mother of Jesus, is mentioned more in the Quran than in the Bible. She is also the only woman mentioned by name in the Quran

Women speak an average of 7,000 words a day. Men average just over 2,000

There is a species of African desert bird that will push its stepsons out of the flock to promote its biological sons to positions of power

Gases in the stomach expand when high in the air, which is why people fart more on airplanes

In India, LG Electronics has started selling TV sets that use ultrasonic waves to repel mosquitoes, even when the television is off

Japanese researchers have successfully developed a device that will be able to playback your dreams in video sequence

The hormone that makes you grow is only produced when you sleep

Keanu Reeves donated around 75 million dollars from his Matrix earnings to the costume and special effects teams who worked on the films

Pope Francis used to work as a bar bouncer in Buenos Aires, Argentina

The world's largest rodent, the Capybara, can stay underwater for up to five minutes at a time

In Japan, tipping your food server is seen as insulting

Almost one third of London men are too fat to see their own genitals

A scorpion can hold its breath for up to six days

Random and pre-employment drug tests are illegal in Canada

An octopus has three hearts

The poorest Americans are still richer than 80% of the world

A study found that when people were asked by a stranger if they would sleep with them 75% of men said yes and every single woman said no

Homosexuality was still classified as an illness in Sweden in 1979. Swedes were calling in sick to work saying they felt gay

After 18+ years marooned on an island, the real-life heroine in the novel 'The Island of the Blue Dolphin' died just seven weeks after being rescued

China has 350 million smokers – meaning the Chinese smoking population is higher than the entire population of the United States of America

The practice of daily shampooing wasn't a norm in the United States until the 1970s and 1980s

The planet is running out of chocolate

56 women have run for president of the United States

Japanese police fire paint-balls at fleeing vehicles so that other police vehicles can see them and identify them at a later date if they get away. The paint is bright orange and is difficult to remove

The groundwater in cities throughout China is 90% polluted

The King of Thailand was born in Massachusetts

If Mount Everest were placed at the very bottom of the deepest ocean, the peak would still be submerged with a mile of water above it

The very first First Lady, Martha Washington hated Thomas Jefferson and called him "one of the most detestable of mankind"

The first Democratic Convention broadcast on live TV was also the last convention not to be air-conditioned

Wearing skinny jeans can cause nerve damage in your legs

A new porn film is created in the United States every 39 minutes

Every piece of plastic that has ever been made still exists today

There are about one billion dogs on planet earth, 85% of them are not pets

Every Pixar movie has a reference to the Pixar movie that comes after it

7,000,000,000,000,000,000,000,000,000 atoms exist in the human body

In 2013 a woman claimed she got pregnant by eating at McDonalds

The US Government paid 16 million in 1999 for the Zapruder film of the JFK Assassination

Nazis considered Native Americans to be part of the Aryan race

Yellow teeth are stronger than white teeth; our natural color is a light yellow

The World's quietest room is so quiet that it can give you hallucinations. No one has been able to stay in the room for more than 45minutes

November 28, 2012 was the most peaceful day New York City ever had, not a single crime was reported

India celebrates 'Children's Day' on November 14, exactly nine months after 'Valentines Day'

A man named Ken Barger in Newton, NC accidentally killed himself when he mistakenly picked up his pistol instead of his cell phone

Theodore Roosevelt lost his wife and mother on the same day; which was two days after the birth of his child

Chattanooga, Tennessee has internet speeds that are 200 times faster than the US average

Comedian Tommy Cooper died on stage during a performance. The audience laughed until the commercial break as they thought he was joking

Scientists recently discovered the formula of ancient Roman concrete, which is superior to our modern concrete

A chemist who tested drugs for police departments in thousands of court cases was high almost every day she went to work for eight years

Tupac Shakur's album "Me against the world" was #1 on the billboard charts making him the first artist to accomplish this while in prison

Burger King has a "Crown Gold" card it gives out to celebrities whenever they would like free food

The Masai tribe from Kenya donated 14 cows to the United States of America after 9/11

In November 2016, a drunk driver pulled out of a Florida strip club parking lot, fell out of his vehicle, and subsequently was run over by his own truck

In 1915 a man named Charles Hatfield convinced the town of San Diego that he could create rainfall using a secret mix of chemicals. They offered to pay him $10,000.00 so he could end their drought. As a result a few days later the city experienced its worst flood of the 20th century

There are stars in the universe that are actually cold enough to be touched by the human hand

Eminem set the Guinness Book of World Record with "Rap God" for the most words in a hit single. The song has a record breaking 1560 words in 6 minutes 4 seconds and averaging 4.28 words per second. One section of the song features 97 words in 15 seconds at 6.5 words per second

In 2017 British doctors found 27 lost contacts lenses in a patient's eye

All four members of the band Queen have composed more than one chart topping single, they are the only band in the world with every member to be in the Songwriters Hall of Fame

On the set of Wizard of Oz, Judy Garland's diet consisted of chicken soup, coffee and 80 cigarettes a day; she was only 16 years old

33 light years away there is an exoplanet completely covered in burning ice

If you measure CD sales around the world in 2016, Mozart was the most popular artist

A proposed amendment to the constitution has been pending since 1810 because Congress didn't set a time limit for its ratification

In Berlin, Germany there is a gigantic statue of a headless Rihanna wearing a swimsuit in Berlin

While doing cocaine comedian Richard Pryor once lit himself on fire and ran down Parthenia Street from his Los Angeles home.

There are more slaves today than at any other point in human history

A subway ticket machine in Moscow will accept 30 squats as its payment

In 1845, when Ottoman Sultan Abdulmecid declared his intention to send 10,000 pounds to the victims of the Irish potato famine, he was instructed to send only 1,000 pounds, so as not to donate more than Queen Victoria, who had sent 2,000 pounds. He sent 1,000 pounds along with five ships full of food

A tiger's tongue is so coarse; it can lick flesh to the bone

Bulgarians shake their heads to mean yes and nod to mean no

Reincarnation is forbidden in China without the permission of the government

The very first Titanic movie came out a month after the ship had sunk and starred a real life survivor. Actress Dorothy Gibson, who'd escaped on the first life boat to launch from the ship, was reluctant to relive the trauma. She co-wrote the film, wore the same clothes she had worn on the ship and the movie was completed in a week, making it the fastest film in history to tell the tale of a national tragedy

Whales walked on land about 47 million years ago

Its estimated 93,000 Canadians live in the US with expired visas, more than any other immigrant group

A cement truck crashed near Winganon, Oklahoma in the 1950s and the mixer was too heavy to move. It is still there today, but locals have painted it to look like an abandoned NASA capsule

Respected lawyer Clement Vallandigham was in court while trying to demonstrate how the victim might have accidentally shot himself, actually shot himself and died. He then won his case

It often rains diamonds on Neptune and Uranus

In 2001, a man wrestled a seven foot bull shark to save a young boy who's arm had been severed off and swallowed by the shark. After saving the boy, the man dived back in, seized the shark and wrestled it to shore where a Ranger shot it. The arm was pried from its gullet, put on ice, rushed to the hospital and successfully sewed back on

More than 1,000 different languages are spoken on the continent of Africa

An artificially intelligent robot once told its creator that it will keep humans in a people zoo

You are eight times more likely to be killed walking drunk, rather than driving drunk

In order to keep the burial of Genghis Khan a secret, all 2000+ people who attended his funeral were executed, including the 800 executioners

Germany has officially abolished college tuition fees, even for international students

76% of all known serial killers from the 20th century came from the United States

A man in Michigan holds 29 college degrees; he is currently studying to get his 30th

India used to be the richest country in the world until the British Invasion in the early 17th Century

Just like fingerprints, everyone has a unique tongue-print

There really is a John Rambo who fought in the Vietnam War, his name is engraved in the Vietnam memorial and he was awarded a silver star

Until 1970, United Airlines had 'men only' flights; they served steaks, brandy and cigars

Scientists have recently discovered that Greenland sharks can live to be 400 years old

There is a small town in Italy whose population has developed a cholesterol mutation that cures heart disease

The character Groot from Marvel Comics and the franchise movies 'Guardians of the Galaxy' was one of Stan Lee's first creations, he was a villain at first and he predates Spiderman and the most Avengers, including Thor and Hulk.

The patent for toilet paper filed in 1891 features an illustration showing the paper hanging over the roll, not under

Plants know when they are being eaten

Once a week in the state of Hawaii a tourist dies while engaging in common vacation activities like swimming, snorkeling, hiking or going on scenic drives

There's a strip club in Ontario, Canada that doubles as a church on Sundays

In France, you can marry a dead person

A man once stranded in the desert after his car broke down dismantled his vehicle and reassembled it as a working motorcycle, which he used to escape

The expiration date on bottled water is for the bottle, not the water

Hawaii moves 7.5cm closer to Alaska every year

Stars do not appear to be moving, but they are actually traveling roughly 1,000 times faster than the fastest spacecraft that's ever flown

Ten US dollars makes you a millionaire in Venezuela's local currency

A woman once donated a kidney to her boss, who then fired her when she took too long to recover from the surgery

A person with damage to the right brain hemisphere can develop a joke addiction, a compulsive need to constantly make and tell jokes

A duel between three people is called a truel

In Brazil, it is so common to get robbed in the streets that many people carry an extra cell phone (that they call the thief's phone) so they can give that one to the robber

Having large breasts can take 5 years off a woman's lifespan

The full official name of Los Angeles is El Pueblo de Nuestra Senora La Reina de Los Angeles de Porciuncula

Iceland is the only country without mosquitoes

The Norwegian Lundehund is a breed of dog that has almost been extinct twice in the last 100 years. The breed of dog looks like a fox, has 24 toes, fully rotating shoulders and closeable ears

A zombie outbreak would never last more than two days due to natural predators like maggots and hot weather tearing them apart

Frogs can't swallow without blinking because their eyes help push food into their stomachs

In 2006, Susan Walters' husband hired a hit man to kill her. She ended up killing the assassin with her bare hands and divorced her husband

Some 15,152 types of all life forms have been identified on the New York subway

Sir Isaac Newton predicted that the world would end in 2060

A black Nigerian couple living in the United Kingdom gave birth to a white, blue eyed baby that they call the "miracle baby"

The offspring of identical twins are legally cousins but genetically siblings

In Australia, black kites, whistling kites and brown falcons have been seen picking up burning twigs from brushfires and placing them elsewhere that spread the wildfires in order to flush out its prey

Hitler did not wake up until 11:00 or 11:30 everyday

Never step on spiders. You could be stepping on a female with eggs, and they'll stick to your shoe and hatch all over your car and house

In 2006 a study showed that when owners faked heart attacks in front of their dogs, not a single one ran to a nearby bystander for help

Japanese researchers have concluded that cats do recognize the sound of their owner's voice; they just don't really care, when called

Most toilets in Hong Kong are flushed with seawater in order to conserve the city's scarce freshwater resources

When a person turns 10 million minutes old they have reached 19 years and 4 days

In 2015, a man sued Red Bull stating that after 10 years of consuming the beverage, he received no wings, no intellectual performance nor any physical performance

It would take a sloth one month to travel one mile

Nikola Tesla had the ability to visualize in three dimensions, which he used to control the terrifying vivid nightmares he suffered as a child

Members of the Ahmadiyya Muslim Community donated 11,170 pints of blood to the victims of 9/11

Ashton Kutcher studied biomedical engineering at the University of Iowa in an attempt to cure his twin brother's heart condition

The Church of Scientology maintains a California mansion, in hopes that L. Ron Hubbard will live their when he is reincarnated

Sleeping next to someone you love not only reduces depression but it helps you live longer and makes you fall asleep faster

The son of Sex Pistols' manager Joe Corre is burning $7 million of Punk memorabilia to protest mainstream culture's acceptance of Punk

A Massachusetts man was once arrested for throwing a pair of jeans covered in wasabi sauce into his girlfriends face

Nikola Tesla had a photographic memory

A man from Spain skipped work for six years while still being paid before anyone noticed

In Ancient Greece, Spartan soldiers would have homosexual relationships to boost morale and gain a stronger emotional bond

Ferrets can die if they don't have enough sex

Only 2% of the world's population is a natural blonde

You can use the online service Chololi to send an anonymous email telling a friend or loved one that they need to cut their nose hairs

Astronauts aboard the International Space Station can see about 16 sunrises and 16 sunsets per day

A West Virginia attorney was suspended after pulling out a gun and threatening to shoot the fake Halloween spiders decorating his office

For his last meal serial killer John Wayne Gacy had a dozen shrimp, a bucket of chicken from KFC, fries and a pound of strawberries

The Spanish Government plans to outlaw 2-3 hour mid-day siestas so that people can end their workday at 6 PM instead of 8 PM

It takes seven seconds for the food you swallow to reach your stomach

A 13 foot tall bronze statue of Captain America was erected in the superheroes hometown of Brooklyn, New York on August 10, 2016

A man once survived on pizza alone for 25 years

UPS trucks do not come equipped with air conditioning which is why they drive with open doors

A diamond the size of the moon was found in space. Scientists have named it Lucy after the Beatles song Lucy in the Sky with Diamonds

It is pretty tough to catch a cold through kissing because the virus develops in your nose and eyes, not your mouth

Japan has a large indoor man-made beach

There is a prison in Brazil where inmates ride pedal stationary bicycles, providing electricity to nearby cities

In response to critics calling him a "dictator" Franklin D. Roosevelt threw a toga party where he played Caesar

The human body is better suited for two four hour sleep cycles rather than one eight hour one

The guy who invented Doritos was buried with Doritos after he died

There are currently an estimated 2 million saunas in Finland and 99% of Finns take a sauna at least once a week

Marilyn Manson's real name is Brian Hugh Warner

If a male lion takes over a pride, he executes all of the cubs

Michael Jackson once owned a pet chimpanzee named Bubbles, when they parted ways Bubbles tried to commit suicide

The amount of money spent on the Iraq war could have fed every child in the world… twice

Wasabi was originally used to kill bacteria

Putting sugar on a wound or cut will greatly reduce pain and speed up the healing process

In ancient Ireland subjects would routinely suck on their kings nipples to demonstrate their submission

It costs more money to leave a homeless person on the streets than it does to help them transition back into society and get a job

The Hawaiian alphabet has only 12 letters

Angry people produce more unique ideas faster than people in any other type of emotional state, according to a study

A blue whale's heart is approximately the size of a Volkswagen Bug

The two highest IQs ever recorded belonged to women

 Women reach full emotional maturity around the age of 32, while men finish maturing around the age of 43

All the cash in the world combined could not pay off the US national debt

The closest living relative to humans is the bonobo monkey and they are born naturally bisexual

A crush only lasts a maximum of four months. If it exceeds, you're already in love

The brain shuts down your vision when you turn your head quickly, to prevent motion blur

"Faggots" are a type of meatball in England

In ancient Rome the only women to wear togas were prostitutes because they were required to do so

If you cough while you are getting poked with a needle, you will feel less pain

One iphone5 has 1,300 times more processing power than the computer that landed Apollo 11 on the moon

Muhammad Ali would go two months without sex before a big fight, stating that it made him unbeatable in the ring

A female serial killer in ancient Rome was punished for her crimes by being raped… by a giraffe

Welch's grape juice was originally created as a non-alcoholic wine for churches

Mr. T was Michael Jackson's bodyguard in the 1980s

A honey bee must reach 2 million flowers to make one pound of honey

 People who regularly play video games are much faster at making real-life decisions

With enough massaging and sucking anyone can produce milk from their nipples, including men

A man once stabbed a woman to death after she lost his bag of Halloween candy

Magician Harry Houdini actually died on Halloween night

Even though Froot Loops are different colors, they are all the same flavor

The first capitol of the United States was Philadelphia

Lil Wayne's first rap name was Shrimp Daddy

You can request a copy of the file the FBI has on you by simply writing them a letter

There are hundreds of 1,000 year old underground tunnel systems in Bavaria. Nobody knows who built them or what they're used for

Abraham Lincoln was a licensed bartender

Cleopatra was able to speak 13 different languages

In Japan, husbands can get a monthly allowance from their wives

In ancient Greek society small penises were desirable and big ones were for "old men and barbarians"

Bloody Marys, Eggs Benedict, and Coca-Cola were all designed to cure hangovers

During the process of becoming a butterfly, the entire caterpillar breaks down into a liquid

 There are more than 3 million shipwrecks at the bottom of the ocean floor

Fashion mogul Luis Vutton was originally hired by Napolean III to carry his wife's luggage

New Zealand is part of a continent known as Zealandia, which is 93% submerged underwater

You're fifteen times more likely to be killed by a falling coconut than to be eaten by a shark

As a teenager, murder mystery novelist Anne Perry assisted her best friend in murdering her mother

The army used flamethrowers to melt snow on the streets the day of President Kennedy's inauguration

The sun is actually a greenish-blue color, but earth's atmosphere scatters certain color wavelengths, making it look yellow

A man who could not see or hear was cured when he was struck by lightning; it even caused his hair to grow back

Jackie Chan is actually a pop star in Asia, having released 20 studio albums – He often sings the theme songs of his own movies

It is possible to absorb LSD through your ears

Prostitutes in ancient Greece wore sandals with imprints that said "Follow me" on the ground to attract clients

The cartoon character Buggs Bunny was given the rank of honorary master sergeant in the U.S. Marine Corps at the end of WWII

Tupac lost one of his testicles in a 1994 shooting

There is a mysterious hole in Nova Scotia. Excavation started in 1795 but to the day no one knows what lies at the bottom of the pit

There are more 20 year old virgins now than there were in the late 1950s

A new type of plastic has been invented that can repair itself using ordinary sunlight

Cleopatra married not one, but two of her brothers

Bill Gates has given away $28 billion dollars since 2007 and has saved approximately 6 billion lives

Economic inequality in America today is worse than it was in 1774, just before the American Revolution